CHINA

VS

USA

A PRIMER FOR SKEPTICS

Other Books by
DAVID W. BLOMSTROM

U.S. Symbols

Geobop's State Symbols

My State Symbols Book

Flag Quest

Grading the States

My Maine State Symbols

What Is Conspiracy?

CHINA VS USA

A PRIMER FOR SKEPTICS

David W. Blomstrom

Edited by Hugh Barker, Reedsy: reedsy.com

Book cover by Andy Meaden, Reedsy: reedsy.com

Interior design by The Book Cover Whisperer:
OpenBookDesign.biz

979-8-9867675-2-9 Paperback

FIRST EDITION

chinavsusa.pro | symbols.geobop.com | whatisconspiracy.com

CONTENTS

CHINA

vs

USA

OPERATOR'S MANUAL

I take great pride in my books, which are well researched and well organized. I've come to favor digital books (aka ebooks, or epubs) because they're insanely portable and have some great features for serious students. Then again, print books do have some advantages of their own (like better interior design).

My ebooks begin with a brief section explaining how each book is organized and how to best use its special features. Since you're reading a paperback version, you don't need any special instructions for the book.

But what about you?

I'm famous for hitting readers over the head with the unvarnished truth, provocative ideas, and—gasp!—conspiracy theories. Your job is to make sure you have your head screwed on straight.

I'm not saying that to be snotty. In today's crazy, propaganda-saturated world, I often have to take time out for a reality check myself.

I'm working on some books exploring the realms of psychology, philosophy, and mind control.

In the meantime, I hope that people who read my books will temporarily suspend their "belief systems" and ponder new ideas that might seem strange at first.

You can always change your mind again after you've read this book.

INTRODUCTION

China! Too big to ignore and too alien to love; what can Americans do but hate it?

In the early twentieth century, China was a humiliated opium addict occupied by Western countries, including the U.S. At the end of World War II, the nation was a shattered third world giant bracing itself for the biggest famine in recorded history. Later headlines told of a long-suffering country that was patiently fixing its problems as it steadily grew in power.

American capitalist tycoons began to cozy up to China as it was transformed into a mecca for corporate whores looking for cheap labor, which they euphemistically called "outsourcing." Stabbed in the back by their own leaders, ordinary American workers could do little but fume. Yet clever corporate propagandists simply insisted that what was best for Big Business was best for America.

However, when the corporate plantation masters suddenly realized that China was about to eat them for lunch, you could almost feel the whiplash.

During his obscenely colorful term as pResident, Donald Trump all but declared war on the "world's factory" in a desperate attempt to curb the rising giant's power. But Trump's bid to hamstring China left him with egg on his face. (Trump's brutal assault on Chinese telecom giant Huawei certainly knocked its celebrated cell phone down a couple notches, but Trump may have injured a lot of U.S. allies in the process, and Huawei is far from down.)

HAVE YOU EVER SEEN A LIST OF THE GOOD THINGS THE WORLD CAN THANK CHINA FOR?

At the same time, the media have obediently stepped up their propaganda campaign, just as they've waged a war of words against other rising powers, or countries that simply refused to kowtow to the American Chamber of Commerce, from Nazi Germany to the Soviet Union to Iran and Libya.

We might recognize six major problems with the anti-Chinese media campaign.

1. Some of China's alleged problems are fabrications.

2. Other Chinese problems are exaggerated.

3. Even authentic problems are seldom put in their proper perspective.

4. Ironically, some of China's most serious problems are largely ignored.

5. The media generally ignore some of the amazingly good things China is doing for the world.

6. The United States' role in China's alleged problems is ignored or whitewashed.

Let me give you some examples...

1. The claim that COVID-19 was created in a laboratory in Wuhan, China is highly likely to be a fabrication. There is powerful evidence that it was actually created in the research facilities at Fort Detrick, Maryland. Until proof is discovered, we also have to consider the possibility that the disease is natural, however.

2. The claim that China is committing "genocide" against the Uyghurs in the autonomous state of Xinjiang is almost certainly a lie as well. Alternatively, it could be

considered an exaggeration, depending on one's definition of *genocide*.

3. The tense relations between China and Taiwan are not a fabrication, and there may be a little exaggeration as well. However, how many Westerners know the history behind the story? How many know that neither the United Nations nor the U.S. regard Taiwan as a sovereign nation?

4. On the other hand, what about China's penchant for building mega-dams around the world? What about its vast fishing fleets that roam the seas far from home? For me, these rank among the most disturbing stories associated with China. So why do Western media whores have so little to say about China's environmental problems?

5. About those good things the media is ignoring ... China is giving Microsoft, Apple and Google some long overdue competition. While Bill Gates, Jeff Bezos and Elon Musk evolve into gazillionaires, China's government holds its billionaires accountable. In addition, China may help Latin America finally escape from Yankee Imperialism. And that's just the tip of the iceberg.

6. When pResident Donald Trump declared war on the Chinese mega-firm Huawei, the media told the public that Huawei's 5G program and smartphone posed a global security risk.

Reality Check: U.S. technology has long ruled the world, and the U.S. has a long track record when it comes to spying on other countries.

And how many people know that U.S. troops joined European powers in occupying China in fairly recent history? The U.S. also took sides in the Chinese Civil War, and China has long been besieged by American spy planes and ships. How many Chinese spy planes or ships do you think have visited the U.S. Pacific Coast?

<u>TOUGH CHOICES</u>

BEFORE ANYONE LABELS ME an apologist for China, let me point out that China is not my favorite country. I would not want to live in China, largely because of its vast population and environmental problems.

In the foreign affairs arena, I would prefer a new world order led by Fidel Castro, Hugo Chavez, or Muammar Gaddafi.

Unfortunately, they're all dead, one (or possibly two) of them murdered by Team USA. That leaves the planet in the hands of the States and/or China, both of which are actually very similar in many respects.

In the end, I think a world ruled by the U.S. is doomed. A world ruled by China might take us down the same path, but what have we got to lose by trying something different? In the short term, they can certainly change the world for the better. The U.S. is nothing more than an anchor stubbornly resisting any kind of progress. (How many times has the U.S. been the lone dissenter or one of a handful of holdouts on international votes of enormous importance, such as the Kyoto Protocols?)

On another note, philosophy students might find this book of interest. Is democracy really better than authoritarianism, and is the U.S. really a democracy to begin with? How much freedom would you trade for security, and how much freedom have Americans already traded for their shallow Facebook friendships?

As you may know, Facebook is banned in China, along with Google and many other websites I wish were banned in the U.S. as well. Some call it censorship, but I agree with those who argue that Google and Facebook are guilty of censorship, along with Orwellian surveillance and global bullying.

Ironically, China took Facebook's "cancel culture" and put it to good use.

EUROPEAN POWERS CARVE UP CHINA IN THIS EERILY
ACCURATE CARTOON.

<u>THE NEW WORLD ORDER</u>

I saved the best for last.

For more than 500 years, the world has been effectively ruled by white people at everyone else's expense. Terms like "Third World country," "developing nation" and "underdeveloped country" are almost synonymous with "non-white country." China itself was once regarded as a Third World country.

During the early twentieth century, a charismatic leader named Adolf Hitler threatened to upset the world order by turning Germany into an amazingly prosperous and powerful country. The Western powers unleashed World War II in an attempt to keep the Germans in their place.

(Yes, Germany invaded Poland, but that little adventure was a can of worms. The bottom line: It was a war between two neighboring countries. It didn't become a world war until the British and French declared war on Germany. I'll have much more to say about this in my book *World War True*.)

However, the Chinese have gone far beyond Germany's National Socialists. So intricate are this new power's economic and technological relations with the U.S., some have begun calling the States a Chinese colony. China could conceivably surpass the U.S. in power without even firing a shot.

Amazingly, the media almost never point out the fact that China threatens the old guard "White Power" regime.

And it isn't just China. Japan and South Korea are among the other Asian countries that are flexing their muscles. Taiwan's Taiwan Semiconductor Manufacturing Company, Limited (TSMC) is the world's most valuable semiconductor company.

China is also pumping money into Latin America and Africa, regions that have long been dominated and exploited by the West. China may have already altered the balance of power in the Middle East; many observers believe the United States' chaotic withdrawal from Afghanistan was forced by the need to reorient our military to deal with the rising power of the Chinese dragon.

Not content to just build valuable infrastructure, China is the only country on the planet that is doing it in the face of U.S. sanctions.

China is doing business with Cuba, Venezuela, Iran and Syria, all of which have been sanctioned by Wall Street. Shame on the United Nations and all the national governments that aren't speaking out and fighting back against this outrageous sitution. By ignoring U.S. sanctions, China is striking a blow for universal freedom. Screw the Statue of Liberty, or better yet, relocate it to Shanghai.

Ironically, and almost unbelievably, the U.S. still has lots of powerful allies, while China appears to be almost alone on the world stage.

Of course, U.S. alliances are often skin-deep. Corrupt governments may align themselves with our country, and weak governments that are afraid of being bombed by the U.S. may also go along, but millions of ordinary citizens around the world hate us.

As China's power and—dare I say it?—virtue continue to win friends around the globe, governments will increasingly support it in many different ways. China will inevitably get more support in the United Nations, for example.

And it's only a matter of time before countries begin openly siding with China, maybe even forming military alliances. In the end, we may be hard pressed to guess if that deafening sucking sound is evidence of America's collapsing economy or a stampede of former allies who are ready to embrace China.

CONVENTIONS

I WOULD LIKE TO offer some brief comments on my writing style and political beliefs.

Though I'm no literary giant, I am proud of my writing style, which has been frequently complimented. I've been published in magazines and even landed a contract for a series of books with a major publisher some three decades ago.

And yet I've had no formal training in the writing arts, and my knowledge of the mechanics of English is frankly lacking. But hey, that's what editors are for, right?

Still, there are a few quirks that I have retained in this book, some of which you will probaby see in most of my books.

I frequently use the word *politix* in place of *politics*. They're pretty much synonymous, except that the former emphasizes the broad spectrum of politics, while the latter is frequently more closely associated with government. I also use politix just to be a little different I guess. In addition, it's good branding for my website Politix. pro and my book *Politix 101*, which will be the foundation of my Introduction to Politix series.

I'm a big believe in honesty, as in calling a spade a spade. I'm also a fierce advocate of accountability, which can include derogatory language.

I've kept the profanity to a minimum in this book, which I don't want to be too politically incorrect. Nevertheless, I routinely use the term "media whore" in lieu of "reporter" or "journalist." Having studied the media very closely, as well as been in their crosshairs as a political activist and candidate for public office, I think "media whore" is far too kind. Callling them journalists or reporters is too damn respectful and dishonest to boot.

Similarly, I just can't bring myself to refer to the top elected official in the United States as a president. I use the term "pResident." In fact, many people refer to the president as "resident," which is synonymous.

Likewise, I often lump Democrats and Republicans together as Demopublicans, and I commonly refer to the general public—especially Americans, who are notoriously apathetic and not politically astute (date I say *not intelligent*?)—as *sheeple*.

WILD CLAIMS

A NUMBER OF EDITORS have taken me to task for saying bad things about prominent people (e.g. George W. Bush, Obama, Hillary Clinton, Bill Gates, etc.) without really making the case for their guilt or evil.

I will try to do better. However, though most of my political books are designed even for novices, I generally assume the people who buy my books will have some knowledge of politics. And with the caliber of America's pResidential candidates going from bad to worse to "shoot me in the head," it should by now be pretty clear that most Demopublicans are scumbags. If you want some dirt on Bill Gates, well, I'm working on a book about that con man, though it probably won't be published until 2024.

Vice versa, I often praise people who most Westerners, particularly Americans, have been brainwashed into thinking were pure evil. My biggest heroes include Malcolm X, Che Guevara, Fidel Castro, Hugo Chavez, and Muammar Gaddafi, who may have been an entire continent's best hope. I even have some good things to say about Adolf Hitler, and before you have a heart attack, take a deep breath and wait for my book *World War True*.

Some people are shocked and offended by my views on historical events, and I have lots to say about conspiracy. For example, I dispute the claims that Hitler started World War II or that he dreamed of world conquest, and I agree with the truthers who believe the 9/11 terrorist attacks were an inside job (aka a "false flag attack").

Many people bristle at the mere mention of the J-word, "Jew." We can trash talk the Chinese and black people, but anyone who merely insults Israel is a racist. And what kind of fool would believe that Jews have more power than other groups of people and are capable of conspiratorial behavior?

That's a topic I won't discuss in any detail in this book, but if you do some research on Nathan Mayer Rothschild, Jacob Schiff, Milton Friedman, Henry Kissinger, Paul Wolfowitz, Jonathan Pollard, Jeffrey Epstein, Harvey Weinstein, Ron Jeremy, Simon Wiesenthal, Mayer Lansky, Sigmund Freud, Ayn Rand, Karl Popper, Ben Shapiro, Bernie Madoff, Michael Milken, Jack Abramoff, or the various "Russian oligarchs" who have attempted to escape Western sanctions by moving to Israel ... well, see how many other ethnic groups can match that record.

Unfortunately, I don't have the luxury of writing detailed reports backing up every one of my claims in each of my books. However, you should be able to find a combination of evidence and logic supporting most of my claims with very little effort. In the meantime, many of these topics will be discussed in a series of books I'm working on.

QUIZ

THIS IS NOT A big, densely worded book. Many middle schoolers could probably handle it.

I wanted to do my best to keep it short and simple, emphasizing important issues rather than lots of minor details.

Just for fun, why not try a short, simple true-or-false quiz before you continue?

Don't feel bad if you don't get a great score. Making mistakes is part of the learning process.

1. Taiwan was originally part of China.

2. Hong Kong was once a British colony.

3. U.S. troops have occupied China.

4. Chinese troops have occupied the U.S.

5. Huawei made the most popular smart phone in the world before the company was hit by U.S. sanctions.

6. The U.S. has nearly 800 military bases in other countries compared to a handful for China.

7. China is practicing genocide against Uyghurs living in Xinjiang.

8. Huawei is the global leader in 5G technology.

9. China has not fought a war since 1979.

10. China and Vietnam have both beaten the U.S. on the battlefield.

(The answers are on the next page.)

<u>ANSWERS TO QUIZ</u>

BELOW ARE THE ANSWERS to the quiz that appeared at the end of the Introduction.

1. **TAIWAN WAS ORIGINALLY PART OF CHINA.**
True. Taiwan was annexed by China in 1683, almost a century before the U.S. even existed.

2. **HONG KONG WAS ONCE A BRITISH COLONY.**
It depends on who you ask. The British insist Hong Kong was part of their sleazy empire. However, they leased it from China. Moreover, the lease was signed at a time when China was groveling at the feet of its Western masters. China's government says it doesn't recognize the treaty that supposedly made Hong Kong a colony.

3. **U.S. TROOPS HAVE OCCUPIED CHINA.**
True. The U.S. sent troops to China during the Boxer Rebellion (1899-1901) and again during World War II.

4. **CHINESE TROOPS HAVE OCCUPIED THE U.S.**
False.

5. **HUAWEI MADE THE MOST POPULAR SMART PHONE IN THE WORLD BEFORE THE COMPANY WAS HIT BY U.S. SANCTIONS.**
Yes, Huawei's smart phone ranked #1 globally before U.S. sanctions shot it down.

6. **THE U.S. HAS NEARLY 800 MILITARY BASES IN OTHER COUNTRIES COMPARED TO A HANDFUL FOR CHINA.**

True, except calling China's military bases "a handful" might be too generous.

7. **CHINA IS PRACTICING GENOCIDE AGAINST UYGHURS LIVING IN XINJIANG.**

That question really can't be answered because no one really knows exactly what the term *genocide* means. If we define it as the large-scale slaughter of a group of people, then the answer is probably FALSE. Western media whores just like to toss around the word genocide for shock value.

8. **HUAWEI IS THE GLOBAL LEADER IN 5G TECHNOLOGY.**

True. Even in the face of U.S. sanctions, it is still beating the competition.

9. **CHINA HASN'T FOUGHT A WAR SINCE 1979.**

True. The Sino-Vietnamese War was China's last war, though it has fought subsequent skirmishes with India.

10. **CHINA AND VIETNAM HAVE BOTH BEATEN THE U.S. ON THE BATTLEFIELD.**

True. Vietnam won a war against the U.S. The most popular movie in China is currently "The Battle at Lake Changjin," which chronicles the bloody Battle of Chosin Reservoir. Though the Americans were eventually able to break free, they were subsequently forced to evacuate the region, marking their complete withdrawal from North Korea.

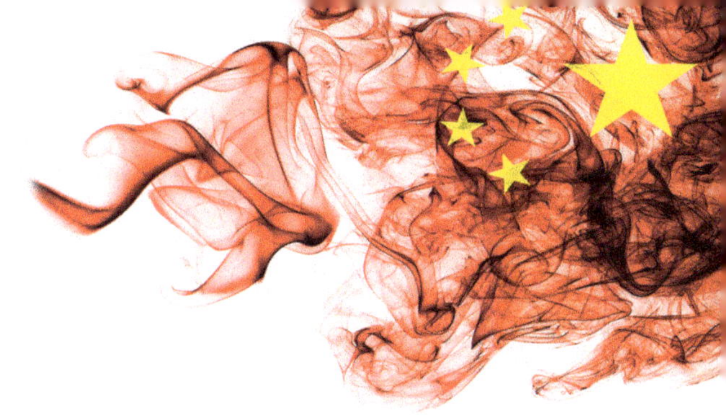

GEOGRAPHY 101

China is a huge country located primarily in eastern Asia. It stretches further to the east than any other mainland Asian country other than Russia.

When measured by land area, China is the third biggest country, after Russia and Canada, and trailed closely by the United States. (The U.S. is slightly bigger than China if we include bodies of water.)

China is bordered by three of Asia's biggest countries—Russia, Kazakhstan and India.

	Country	Square Miles	...Kilometers
The 10 Biggest Countries			
1	Russia	6,601,665	17,098,242
2	Canada	3,855,101	9,984,670
3	China	3,747,877	9,706,961
4	United States	3,618,783	9,372,610
5	Brazil	3,287,955	8,515,767
6	Australia	2,969,906	7,692,024
7	India	1,269,345	3,287,590
8	Argentina	1,073,518	2,780,400
9	Kazakhstan	1,052,089	2,724,900
10	Algeria	919,595	2,381,741

China, Mongolia, North Korea, South Korea and Japan are commonly classified as East Asian countries.

The bulk of East Asia consists of China and Russia, with Mongolia sandwiched in between. Dangling from northeastern China is the Korean peninsula, which is divided into North and South Korea. Farther east is the island nation of Japan and the island of Taiwan, which was historically part of the Chinese empire.

China, South Korea, Taiwan and Japan are all economic powerhouses. Japan boasted the world's second biggest economy until it was eclipsed by China in 2009. And, as already mentioned, Taiwan is the world's biggest producer of silicon chips/semiconductors, which are now widely considered more valuable than fossil fuels.

WHITE PEOPLE BEWARE:
THOSE CRAZY RICH ASIANS ARE GETTING RICHER.

A CLOSER LOOK

EASTERN CHINA IS A land of rich agricultural plains and moderate climate. Western China, on the other hand, is far more mountainous, with vast deserts at the mercy of Siberian winter blasts.

The political map is a little more complex.

The People's Republic of China (PRC) administers 34 provincial-level divisions or first-level divisions, including 22 provinces, five autonomous regions, four municipalities, and two special administrative regions and one claimed province.

The map below lists some of China's more notable cities.

TROUBLE SPOTS

THE MAP BELOW DEPICTS eight of China's most controversial areas.

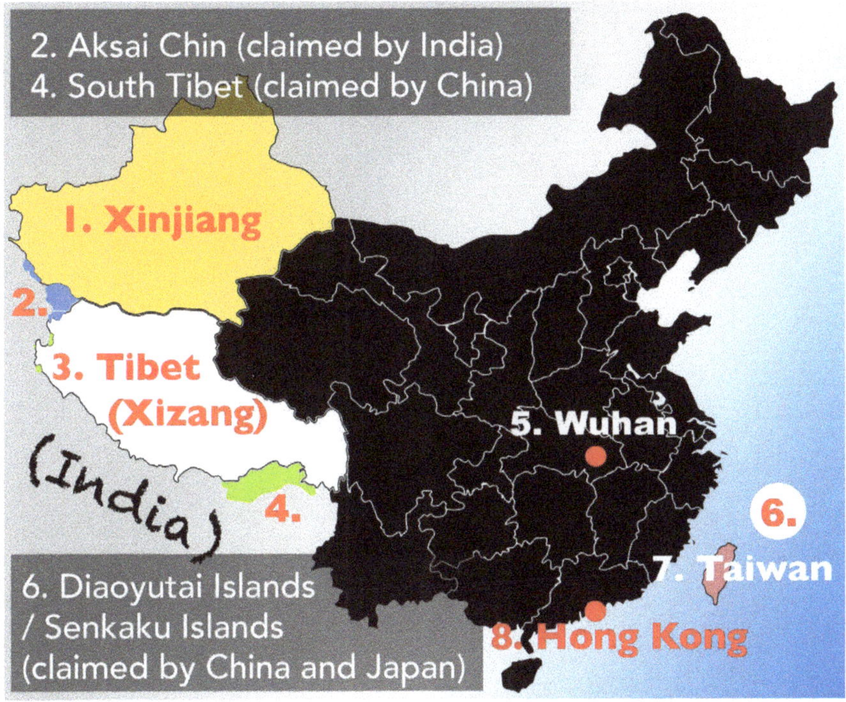

Portions of the Chinese empire that are commonly portrayed as trouble spots include Hong Kong, Xinjiang and Tibet on the mainland. Maritime flash points consist primarily of Taiwan, the Senkaku Islands and the South China Sea, all of which are claimed to some extent by China.

This book features separate chapters focusing on Hong Kong, Xinjiang, Tibet, Taiwan and the South China Sea.

Hong Kong was a British colony until relatively recently. Xinjiang and Tibet are culturally distinct regions that were absorbed into the Chinese empire longer ago.

The island of Taiwan was declared a sovereign nation by the Nationalists after they lost China's civil war.

The coronavirus associated with COVID-19 allegedly

originated in the city of Wuhan, according to a large portion of the Western media.

THE SOUTH CHINA SEA IS A PARTICULARLY COMPLEX GEOPOLITICAL PROBLEM.

Aksai Chin and South Tibet are claimed by both China and India, leading to friction between the two countries.

Bordering China on the south are the countries that make up Southeast Asia, which was long a battlefield for European and U.S. colonial powers. West of Southeast Asia is India, which might be described as America's whore. More precisely, the U.S. has propped up India as a bulwark against China.

Russia and India have nuclear weapons, as do two other countries that border China—Pakistan and North Korea.

RUSSIA IS ONE OF FOUR COUNTRIES BORDERING CHINA
THAT HAVE NUCLEAR WEAPONS..

India is bordered on the west by its long-time adversary, Pakistan. Bordering Pakistan on the west is Afghanistan, another country that, like China, has been occupied by the U.S. and the British, along with the Soviet Union.

A LITTLE PERSPECTIVE

FOR A LITTLE PERSPECTIVE, compare China to the U.S.

The U.S. is bordered by just two countries, Canada and Mexico, both of which are virtual puppet states. The U.S. is the only nuclear power in the Western Hemisphere. No Asian country's military has occupied any country in the Western Hemisphere apart from a brief Japanese incursion into Alaska's Aleutian Islands during World War II. During the 18th and 19th centuries, what is now Alaska, along with much of the Pacific Coast region south into California, was claimed by Russia.

RUSSIAN AMERICA WAS THE NAME OF THE RUSSIAN COLONIAL POSSESSIONS IN NORTH AMERICA FROM 1799 TO 1867.

However, the Russians retreated across the Bering Strait when Alaska was sold to the U.S. in 1867.

In plain English, China's political geography is far more complex and volatile than Club USA's.

It almost seems as if Nature has taken sides against China as well.

East of China is the so-called First Island Chain, which consists of the Japanese archipelago, Taiwan, the Philippines, and the islands of Indonesia. Traditionally allied with the U.S., these islands form a perimeter partially blocking China's access to the broader Pacific Ocean.

Beyond the First Island Chain is the Second Island Chain, which serves as the United States' second strategic defensive line in the West Pacific. The Second Island Chain includes the Mariana Islands (most notably Guam, with its heavily fortified military base) and the western Caroline Islands (Yap and Palau), extending to Western New Guinea far to the southwest. The chain serves as the eastern maritime boundary of the Philippine Sea.

For perspective, consider once again this North American map.

There are no major islands blocking U.S. access to the Pacific, Atlantic or Arctic oceans.

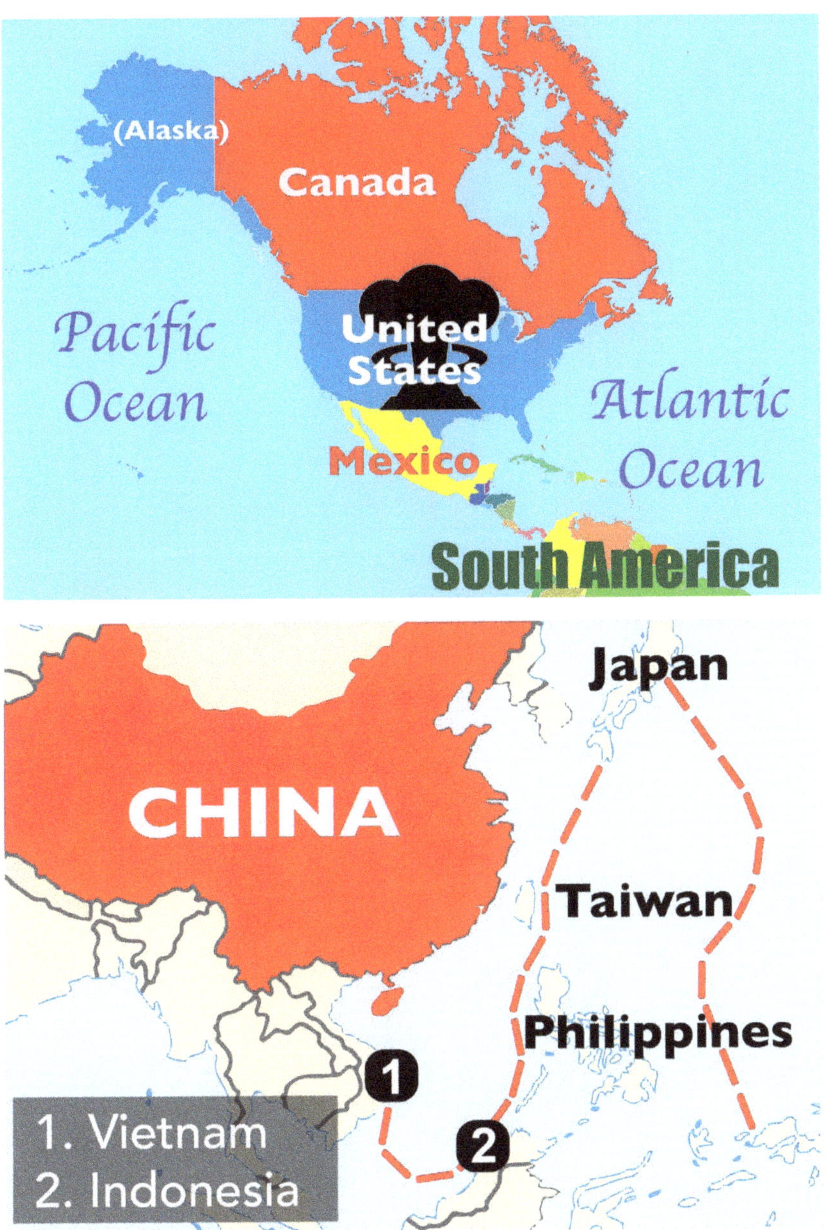

By contrast, China has access to just one ocean, and it's partially blocked by two island chains.

China
Pacific
Ocean
USA

No, I'm not going to overwhelm you with the history of the Chinese people stretching back thousands of years.

We all know that Chinese civilization has deep and fabulously complex roots. To put it in perspective, we might say the story of civilization has two notable origins, one in the Middle East, the other in Eastern Asia.

However, there is one important point I'd like to make about ancient China.

When we focus on ancient Persia, Greece and Rome, there is a notable emphasis on empire building. The Persians ruled what is now Greece until Alexander the Great went on the warpath, carving out a huge empire. Perhaps no more legendary military commander ever lived.

Alexander the Great was a far better example of a warmonger than Adolf Hitler, yet he's honored far and wide. For instance, Alexandria, Egypt, is named in his honor.

The Greeks, of course, were eventually conquered by the Romans, who built an enormous empire comprising much of Europe and portions of North Africa and the Middle East. Along the way, the Romans utterly destroyed their North African rival, Carthage.

Another notable non-European empire arose on the plains of Mongolia, where Genghis Khan would find immorality as a conqueror in the tradition of Alexander the Great. Coming into power in the 12th century, Genghis Khan and his followers conquered most of Eurasia, including China.

SPLENDID ISOLATION

THE STRIKING THING ABOUT ancient China was its relative divorce from the business of empire building.

Plenty of wars were fought between early Chinese states before a greater Chinese state was forged. But the Chinese never conquered Southeast Asia, India or Japan. They never tried to colonize Europe or the Middle East.

On the contrary, the Chinese famously regarded non-Chinese peoples as barbarians to be shunned. They could be traded with, but carefully. The Great Wall of China was built to protect the Chinese people from the barbarians that swirled around their splendid civilization. However, it didn't stop the Mongols.

Under the leadership of Kublai Khan, the Mongols conquered China in the 13th century after an effort spanning six decades.

Before the Mongol conquest, China was the leading maritime

power in the years 1400–1433, when Chinese shipbuilders began to build massive ocean-going junks. This was shortly before Christopher Columbus made his historic landfall in the New World in 1492.

Admiral Zheng He led seven expeditions in the Western Ocean, commanding expeditionary treasure voyages to Southeast Asia, the Indian subcontinent, Western Asia, and East Africa from 1405-1433. According to legend, his larger ships carried hundreds of sailors on four decks and were almost twice as long as any wooden ship ever recorded.

Yet the world would soon be controlled by European navigators, while the much bigger Chinese ships disappeared into history.

<u>COLONIALISM</u>

PORTUGUESE SEAFARERS WERE MAKING their mark on the world map even before Christopher Columbus made landfall in the New World near the end of the 15th century (1492).

A BRITISH STEAMSHIP ATTACKING A FLEET OF CHINESE WAR JUNKS DURING THE FIRST OPIUM WAR (1839-1842).

Europeans would effectively rule the world for more than 500 years, and not even mighty China would be spared.

Though several European powers preyed on a largely helpless China, the star of the show was Great Britain, which famously fought a series of Opium Wars designed to further weaken and humiliate China. Imagine using drugs as a weapon for empire building.

The years 1899-1901 saw an ill-fated Boxer Rebellion (aka Boxer Uprising, Boxer Insurrection or the Yihetuan Movement), which was smashed by what could almost be described as a forerunner of the United Nations.

Named for its members' skills in Chinese martial arts, the Boxer Rebellion started after the Sino-Japanese War of 1895. Villagers in Northern China resented the extension of special privileges to Christian missionaries. In 1898, Northern China also experienced several natural disasters, including the Yellow River flooding and droughts. Boxers blamed these disasters on foreign and Christian influence.

In 1899, the Boxers began destroying foreign property and attacking Christian missionaries and Chinese Christians. In June 1900, Boxer fighters who believed themselves invulnerable to foreign weapons converged on Beijing. They were countered by an Eight-Nation

Alliance of American, Austro-Hungarian, British, French, German, Italian, Japanese and Russian troops.

With 20,000 armed troops, the Eight-Nation Alliance broke the siege and began plundering the capital and the surrounding countryside, at the same time executing people suspected of being Boxers. China's embattled government was forced to pay a huge punitive fee worth more than its annual tax revenue.

And so China was the scene of ongoing misery even before the two world wars. During World War II, China was invaded by Japanese troops, whose atrocities were perhaps most keenly associated with an orgy of rape, torture and murder that came to be epitomized by the Rape of Nanking.

The U.S. helped China deal with the Japanese, but how could the U.S. refrain from taking sides in China's ongoing civil war? Surely, the U.S. couldn't support Communism. The logical ally was the nationalist Republic of China (ROC). And when the Communists won, the U.S. was reluctant to treat the victor as a respectable head of state.

FROM COMMUNISM TO SUCCESS

CHINA WAS WRACKED BY a bloody civil war that was fought intermittently from 1929-1947. The war pitted the Nationalists (Kuomintang), who were supported by the U.S., against the Communists.

Eventually, the Communists won, and Mao Zedong became China's leader. The Nationalists fled to Taiwan, from where they claimed to be China's true government in exile.

"Chairman Mao," as Zedong was popularly known, was a confusing character. As the founder of modern China (more precisely the founding father of the People's Republic of China), he is still treated with some reverence. However, there are some skeletons in his closet—millions of them, in fact.

Under Mao's Great Leap Forward (1958-1961), China experienced the Great Chinese Famine, which they call The Difficult Three Year Period. Agricultural collectivization, which prohibited private ownership of farms, along with natural droughts, caused the starvation of an estimated 15 to 40 million people.

It is commonly said that policy mistakes were the main cause of the starvation. Collectivization, along with the forced use of unproven farming techniques, yielded a bitter harvest. Some have also claimed that Mao put a bounty on birds, which he believed were eating too much valuable grain. Poor farmers obligingly slaughtered birds by the millions, resulting in an insect explosion that proved ruinous.

Yet another Mao-inspired policy that proved disastrous was the Cultural Revolution (1966-1976). The movement was an attempt to preserve Chinese Communism by purging China of all that was bourgeois or Western, along with traditional Chinese culture. Aside from trashing China's priceless culture, the Cultural Revolution led to a death toll for which estimates range from hundreds of thousands to 20 million.

Before I continue, let me say that I do not hate communism or Chairman Mao. I do not believe communism is inherently evil, though I don't think it's a good fit for most (if any) modern nations, either. It's hard to judge Mao when so much of his life is wrapped in mystery. I view him as a tragically flawed figure who did some wonderful things and some terrible things. However, I could be wrong; maybe he was one of history's biggest monsters, period.

At any rate, I would tend to agree with those who believe that communism didn't do much for China, beyond unifying the country and driving U.S. forces back during the Korean War.

One person who probably agreed with me was Deng Xiaoping, who served as China's paramount leader from 1978-1989.

Xiaoping liked to quote an old proverb—"It doesn't matter whether a cat is black or white, if it catches mice it is a good cat." In other words, Xiaoping was more interested in results than ideology. He wasn't afraid to experiment with capitalism.

Under Xiaoping's leadership, China's economy evolved into a hybrid between communism and capitalism, and the country began to move forward. A so-called "mixed" economy has also proved popular in Latin America in recent years. Perhaps capitalism and communism are both too extreme.

With China's economic power and standard of living increasing every year, it was a different country by the time Xi Jinping became the paramount leader in 2012, and Jinping would change it yet again. Whereas previous leaders were relatively quiet, Jinping embraced a more assertive foreign policy. Suddenly, Americans were predicting the dates by which the U.S. would be eclipsed by China's economy and military.

LEFT TO RIGHT: MAO ZEDONG, DENG XIAOPING, AND JI XINPING
(CC—SEE CREDITS)

NEO-COLONIALISM

TODAY, NO U.S., EUROPEAN or Japanese troops are stationed on Chinese soil. China's treasury is no longer pillaged by Westerners, nor are the Chinese forced to serve their masters as opium addicts.

And yet China is still treated with notable contempt. It is surrounded by states allied with the U.S.—from Japan to Taiwan, the Philippines to India—that weaken China's military security even as the U.S. continually builds up its own security thousands of miles from home.

The U.S. has long freely operated spy planes, ships, submarines and satellites near and over Chinese territory. Yet how many Chinese spy planes and ships have ever operated off the coast of California?

CHINESE PEOPLE

China has long been the most populous country in the world. In 2020, it had a population of slightly more than 1.4 billion.

Neighboring India was second, with just under 1.4 billion. A population of 331 million puts the U.S. in third place. That's less than one quarter of China's population.

Just as the United States has long been dominated by white people of European ancestry, so is China dominated by the Han Chinese (commonly called "Chinese"), who currently comprise approximately 92% of its mainland population. Chinese people have spread around the world and constitute the world's largest ethnic group, comprising approximately 18% of the global human population.

One notable difference between the Chinese and Americans is the fact that the Chinese didn't emigrate from another continent.

They are native Asians, though they have spread beyond their original native lands.

THE RESIDENTS OF TAIWAN ARE VARIOUSLY CALLED CHINESE OR TAIWANESE.

The People's Republic of China officially recognizes 56 native Chinese ethnic groups.

China's five largest ethnic minorities, with populations of approximately ten million or more, are the Zhuang, Hui, Manchus, Uyghurs and Miao. The Yi, Tujia, Tibetans and Mongols each have populations between five and ten million.

Approximately 2% of Taiwan's population is made up of in-digenous peoples, some of whom have lived in Taiwan for up to 6,000 years prior to the colonization of Taiwan by China in the 17th century. The Republic of China (ROC) recognizes 17 native Taiwanese ethnic groups, along with ethnic groups that immigrated from Mainland China and Southeast Asia.

TWO CHINAS

Cut China in half diagonally, and you wind up with two very different Chinas. More than 90% of the population lives in the eastern half, which is a land of fertile plains. The great majority of people who live here are Han Chinese.

To the west, the land is far more rugged and the climate more severe. In the southwest, the Himalayas form an enormous rain shadow that stretches across the Tibetan plateau and the arid Gobi and Taklamakan deserts.

This is China's Wild West, and the relatively small number of people who live here include many of the country's more conspicuous minorities.

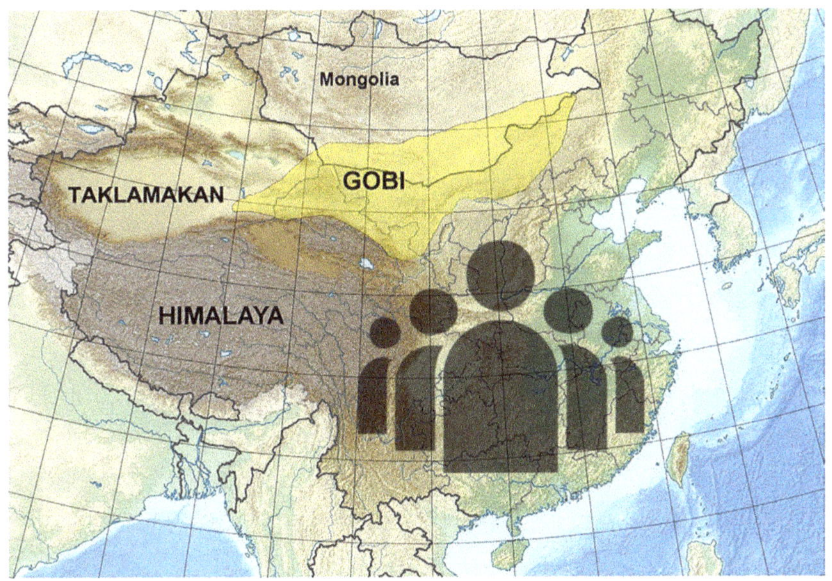

(CC—SEE CREDITS)

However, there is a drive to settle and develop these wilder regions, just as the American West was settled by Europeans. In the meantime, there will inevitably be suspicions and tensions between China's western minorities and the eastern settlers who continue to pour into their lands.

PERSPECTIVE

THE UNITED STATES IS theoretically a democracy with a population of approximately one third of a billion people. It has some rather horrendous problems, ranging from government and corporate corruption to crime, poverty and homelessness.

The rise of hyper-disgusting political leaders like George W. Bush, Obama, Hillary Clinton, Donald Trump and Joe Biden is striking evidence of the collapse of the U.S. electoral system, the collapse of democracy itself.

IT'S NO SECRET THAT CORPORATIONS CONTROL THE U.S. GOVERNMENT, BUT THEY CERTAINLY DON'T CONTROL CHINA'S GOVERNMENT.

China has more than four times as many people as the U.S. Yet it arguably has less corporate corruption, which is probably one reason it has done so much more to alleviate poverty.

Still, there are political and ethnic tensions within China, just as there are in other countries. However, China's enormous population, combined with a history of foreign occupation and exploitation, make stability an especially urgent priority.

GOVERNMENT

According to Wikipedia's article "Government of China,"

"The government of the People's Republic of China (Chinese: 中华人民共和国政府; pinyin: *Zhōnghuá Rénmín Gònghéguó Zhèngfǔ*) is collectively the state authority in the People's Republic of China (PRC) under the exclusive political leadership of the Chinese Communist Party (CCP). It consists of legislative, executive, military, supervisory, judicial, and procuratorial branches."

Of course, the word that sums it up for most Westerners is "Communist."

In the West, we're mostly taught that communism is evil, and capitalism is good. And lest you think that's a rational comparison, remember the slogan that adorns U.S. currency: "In God We Trust."

To cut to the chase, there are two arguments we need to tackle here...

1. Is communism good or bad?
2. Is China really a communist country?

The second question is a no brainer; the answer is "of course not."

According to the Hurun Global Rich List 2021, China has 1,058 billionaires, more than any other country. In comparison, the U.S. has 696 billionaires. Just to rub it in, consider this article: "Beijing now has more billionaires than any city" (Justin Harper, BBC News, April 8, 2021).

I'm not the foremost authority on Karl Marx, widely regarded as the father of communism, but I don't think he envisioned a proletariat studded with billionaires.

Verdict: China is no more a true communist state than the U.S. is a true democracy. that would appear to render the first question moot.

On the other hand, China's leaders must have some communist credentials. And we can't deny communism's historical role in China.

The Chinese Civil War pitted the Kuomintang (KMT)-led government of the Republic of China (ROC) against the forces of the Chinese Communist Party (CCP) from 1927 to 1949, when the communists gained control of the mainland. Given the ruthlessness with which capitalistic Western powers had exploited China, it isn't hard to understand why the people welcomed communism as an alternative.

Whether or not communism was a good choice for China is a hard question to answer. Though I don't think communism is inherently evil, I don't think it's the best fit for most modern nations, either. Then again, it could be a good short-term solution for countries with especially dire problems, and China was up to its eyeballs in dire problems during the first half of the twentieth century.

Let's just say that socialism (which may or may not include communism) and capitalism both have their pros and cons, and China is not a true communist state any more than the U.S. is an authentic beacon of capitalism (or democracy).

China's government is commonly criticized as being authoritarian.

That's probably a fair assessment, bearing in mind that the U.S. government is also quite authoritarian. But China's government is widely branded as something even worse. Its policies in Tibet and Xinjiang are sometimes described as genocidal, and why can't China leave Taiwan alone?

However, while it is hard to determine exactly what's happening in Tibet and Xinjiang, it can't be half as bad as what the U.S. did in Iraq, Afghanistan and Libya. And why can't the U.S. leave Cuba, Venezuela, Iran and Syria alone?

The Chinese government's website, by the way, is www.gov.cn, or see the English version @ www.gov.cn/english.

MILITARY

The U.S. military is clearly a global affair. After all, the U.S. has nearly 800 military bases in other countries, and it has invaded, occupied and destroyed countries around the world.

But what about China?

China fought against the U.S. in the Korean War. It later fought with Vietnam. It has also had a few military skirmishes with India.

And that's just about the end of the story.

In fact, China's military is overwhelmingly defensive. It is designed primarily to protect it from foreign enemies; primarily the U.S. China's military is very similar to the Great Wall of China, which was similarly defensive.

Unfortunately, the U.S. keeps pushing and pushing, and it was inevitable that China would respond.

In recent years, China has poured ever more resources into its military, quickly building up one of the most powerful forces on the planet.

China still only has three aircraft carriers, but it has more ships in total than the U.S. Navy. China has an enormous armada of missiles, and it is a leader in the development of hypersonic missiles.

Although the U.S. is still the global leader in nuclear weapons, China is rapidly expanding its nuclear deterrent.

China is also pushing the envelope with aircraft, drones, satellites and artificial intelligence.

Curiously, China still has amazingly few foreign military bases. The most notable is perhaps a base in Djibouti, East Africa.

China may be planning to acquire military bases in a few other countries, including Cambodia and Pakistan. In 2021, there were reports that the U.S. had nixed a secret plan for the construction of a Chinese military facility at a port in Abu Dhabi, in the United Arab Emirates.

Of special interest is a rumored quest for a military base on Africa's west (Atlantic) coast, which is much closer to the U.S. than China is. Some sources say China has already acquired a site in Equatorial Guinea.

While the U.S. military is overwhelmingly offensive in nature, China's budding military adventurism appears designed primarily to protect its investments in its ambitious One Belt One Road global infrastructure program.

I wish Libya could have had the protection of a Chinese military base. In a similar vein, I'm hoping to see a Chinese military base built in Iran one day soon. That would give the U.S. government and Israel something to choke on.

DOMESTIC AFFAIRS

This section focuses primarily on areas within China or on its borders.

THE ID KAH MOSQUE AT KASHGAR IS CHINA'S BIGGEST MOSQUE.

XINJIANG (UYGHURS)

"KOKBAYRAQ" FLAG, USED BY THE UYGHURS AS A SYMBOL OF THE EAST TURKESTAN INDEPENDENCE MOVEMENT. THE CHINESE GOVERNMENT PROHIBITS USING THE FLAG WITHIN CHINA.

Making up China's northwest corner is Xinjiang, a landlocked autonomous region bordering Tibet on the north. A land of rugged beauty, Xinjiang has about 25 million inhabitants spread across more than half a million square miles (1.6 million square km). Only about 9.7% of Xinjiang's land area is considered fit for human habitation. Among the diverse ethnic groups that call this harsh land home are the Uyghurs, China's most familiar Muslims.

The territory came under the rule of China's Qing dynasty in the 18th century. Since 1949 and the Chinese Civil War, it has been part of the People's Republic of China.

From the 1900s to the 2010s, the East Turkestan independence movement, separatist conflict and the influence of radical Islam have resulted in unrest in the region, with occasional terrorist attacks and clashes between separatist and government forces.

In response, China's government has allegedly set up internment camps where its Muslim population is pressured into abandoning the faith through thought reform. Some reports claim one million Uyghurs are currently being held in re-education camps.

There have also been claims of forced birth control among Uyghur women.

Exactly what is the truth is hard to say.

In July 2019, 22 countries—Australia, Austria, Belgium, Canada, Denmark, Estonia, Finland, France, Germany, Iceland, Ireland, Japan, Latvia, Lithuania, Luxembourg, the Netherlands, New Zealand, Norway, Spain, Sweden, Switzerland, and the UK—sent a letter to the UN Human Rights Council, criticizing China for its mass arbitrary detentions and other violations against Muslims in China's Xinjiang region. However, on July 12, a group of 37 countries submitted a similar letter in defense of China's policies: Algeria, Angola, Bahrain, Belarus, Bolivia, Burkina Faso, Burundi, Cambodia, Cameroon, Comoros, Congo, Cuba, Democratic Republic of the Congo, Egypt, Eritrea, Gabon, Kuwait, Laos, Myanmar, Nigeria, North Korea, Oman, Pakistan, Philippines, Qatar, Russia, Saudi Arabia, Somalia, South Sudan, Sudan, Syria, Tajikistan, Togo, Turkmenistan, United Arab Emirates, Venezuela, and Zimbabwe.

Western media whores' penchant for collectively categorizing alleged questionable practices towards the Uyghur as genocide seems exaggerated at best.

HOW CAN A GOVERNMENT BE GUILTY OF GENOCIDE WHEN THE TARGETED GROUP'S POPULATION GROWTH IS HIGHER THAN THAT OF THE MAJORITY?

Doesn't the term genocide refer to the attempted destruction of an entire race? In fact, the word *genocide* has been manipulated to such an insane degree as to become nearly meaningless.

This isn't to say the Uyghurs aren't victims of oppression, but what is the whole truth?

And isn't it awfully hypocritical for the U.S. and its allies to campaign against alleged Chinese genocide directed at a mostly Muslim ethnic group even while the U.S. has waged war against Muslims in Afghanistan, Iraq, Syria and Libya?

Looking even closer to home, how does the situation in Xinjiang compare to the treatment of Native Americans in the U.S., where entire tribes and cultures have been eradicated? They call it the American Holocaust for a reason.

In the meantime, the U.S. spearheaded a "diplomatic boycott" of the 2022 Winter Olympics in Beijing, an effort boosted by images and posters linking the games to genocide.

In that spirit, wouldn't it be fair to begin boycotting U.S. sports spectacles over that country's treatment of Iran, Syria, Cuba and Venezuela? How about an Olympic boycott that points a finger at America's burgeoning homeless population?

With a documented history of at least 2,500 years, a succession of people and empires have vied for control over all or parts of Xinjiang. They may very well spend another 1,000 years thrashing out the details.

TIBET

Tibet is one of the most enigmatic regions on the planet. Commonly referred to as "the roof of the world," it's home to rugged high-altitude plains, yaks and remote Buddhist monasteries.

Chinese dynasties have had various levels of control over Tibet since the Yuen Dynasty (1271-1368). The relationship between China and Tibet is said to have been friendly at that time.

CENTURIES AGO, TIBETANS MADE INCURSIONS INTO CHINA AS THEY SOUGHT TO EXPAND THEIR EMPIRE. HOWEVER, THE CHINESE TURNED THE TABLES AND EVENTUALLY MADE TIBET THEIR OWN.

However, Tibet was largely independent after the Ming Dynasty (1368-1644) lost influence there.

The Qing Dynasty (1644-1912) reasserted control over Tibet.

However, rulers were forced to send troops to assert their control towards the end of the dynasty.

In 1903, Tibet was invaded by Great Britain, which ruled neighboring India as a colony. (The skirmishes between China and India that continue today are largely the legacy of the "colonial border" between Tibet and India.) Subsequently a complex deal also involving Russia led to the return of Chinese rule. However, when the Qing Dynasty fell in 1911, Tibet expelled all Chinese troops and refused to submit to the new Chinese government.

When China's civil war was finally over, the country's leaders turned their attention to Tibet one more time. Its 37 years of independence came to an end when Tibet was once again invaded by China in 1950. At that time, Great Britain considered Tibet a part of China.

The new government negotiated a Seventeen Point Agreement with the newly enthroned 14th Dalai Lama's government, affirming China's sovereignty but granting the area autonomy. However, the Dalai Lama later repudiated the agreement.

Though long ruled by China, Tibet remains uniquely Tibetan. It doesn't seem possible that it could or should be controlled by a distant government in the lowlands far below.

Is it appropriate for China to occupy Tibet? What value does it see in such a harsh, remote wasteland? And how fairly are the Tibetan people treated?

Tibet is probably seen in part as a bulwark against India, a country propped up by the U.S. as an enemy of China. Loosely speaking, one might argue that the U.S. is at least partly responsible for China's grip on Tibet.

However, Tibet also possesses a highly valuable resource: water. The sources of some of southern Asia's greatest rivers lie among the snows of Tibet. China has begun building dams on some of these rivers, a practice I find utterly abhorrent.

And that's just about all I know about Tibet. I doubt that China's government is telling the outside the world the whole truth about Tibet, but I'm sure the West isn't telling people the truth, either.

HAVE TIBETANS BEEN TREATED WORSE THAN THE LAKOTAS AND OTHER U.S. INDIAN TRIBES?

A book of this nature would be incomplete without a reference to Tibet. However, Tibet is a complex subject and I certainly don't claim to be an expert on its history or culture.

In some respects, Tibet reminds me of my native West Dakota, a remote grassland long ruled by the Dakota people (aka Sioux) but today controlled by the United States.

Perhaps we can just describe Tibet as a majestic victim of geopolitics.

China's critics like to hold up Hong Kong as an example of a democratic spitfire being cruelly kicked in the shins by its authoritarian Communist Chinese masters.

How quickly they forget that Hong Kong long existed as a British colony. The colonial flag pictured on the left represented Hong Kong from 1959-1977.

Even before Hong Kong began to show its later commercial prowess, it was a pawn in the Opium Wars, hardly England's finest gesture towards the Chinese.

By the early 1990s, Hong Kong had established itself as a global financial center and shipping hub.

Diplomatic negotiations with China resulted in the 1984 Sino-British Joint Declaration, in which the United Kingdom agreed to transfer the colony in 1997. In return, China promised to guarantee Hong Kong's economic and political systems for 50 years after the transfer.

There were a few bumps in the road. Amid uncertainty over the future, over half a million people left the territory during the period 1987-1996. The government was forced to use substantial foreign exchange reserves to maintain the Hong Kong dollar's currency peg during the 1997 Asian financial crisis. The recovery was muted by an H5N1 avian flu outbreak and a housing surplus. This was followed by the 2003 SARS epidemic, during which the territory experienced its most serious economic downturn.

Then there were the political protests. In June 2019, mass protests erupted in response to a proposed extradition amendment bill permitting the extradition of fugitives to Taiwan. Protesters argued that criminals might be extradited to mainland China. The protests are said to have been the largest in Hong Kong history, with organizers claiming to have attracted more than three million Hong Kong residents.

The protests also took a nasty turn, veering into violent riots that saw protesters and law enforcement officials alike injured. The timing was suspicious, coinciding with pResident Donald Trump's trade war and striking shortly before a global coronavirus pandemic.

RENT-A-RIOT

WHO WERE THESE VIOLENT protesters? Did they really represent Hong Kong? Were they trying to goad Chinese authorities into over-reacting, giving the Western media an opportunity to paint them as authoritarian Communist thugs?

According to Wikipedia, "Hong Kong is governed by a hybrid regime that is not fully representative of the population."

MANY OBSERVERS OPINED THAT HONG KONG'S MOST VALUABLE
PROTESTER WAS U.S. SERETARY OF STATE MIKE POMPEO
(LEFT). (CC—SEE CREDITS)

As a long-time political activist based in Seattle, Washington, I can only wonder how the two cities compare. Seattle is a downright racist, two-class city ruled by the rich for the rich. Surely, Hong Kong has nothing that compares with Seattle's army of homeless people. Sex trafficking is also an issue in both cities.

FLOURISHING METROPOLIS

HONG KONG CURRENTLY RANKS as the world's 35th-largest economy. The Hong Kong Stock Exchange is the seventh-largest in the world. Hong Kong is also the tenth largest trading entity in exports and imports. Hong Kong boasts the world's seventh busiest container port and the busiest airport for international cargo.

HONG KONG'S LARGEST EXPORT MARKETS ARE MAINLAND CHINA AND THE U.S.

In all honesty, Hong Kong holds little attraction for me. It is one of the most densely populated places in the world. One of the most developed cities in the world, it also boasts some of the most expensive housing (along with plenty of shacks). More than 90% of Hong Kong's food is imported.

But if I'm looking for an example of authoritarianism and human rights abuses, Hong Kong is about the last place I'll look. How can Hong Kong even begin to compare with Afghanistan, Iraq, Syria, Libya and the many other places the authoritarian U.S. has cruelly destroyed?

In the meantime, there are many intriguing comparisons to be made between the corporate ghetto of Seattle and the glitzy high-rise of Hong Kong. And in both cases this exists alongside plenty of poverty, deprivation and misery.

TAIWAN

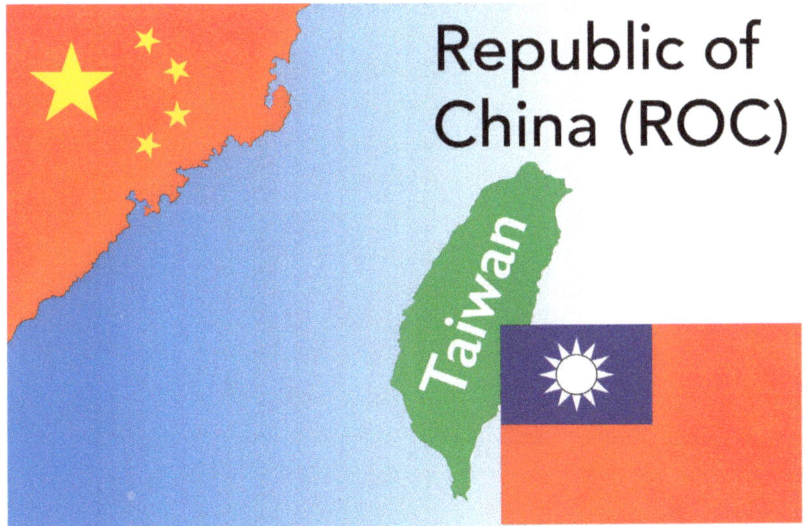

Forget Hong Kong, Tibet and the South China Sea. When it comes to China, the elephant in the living room is Taiwan.

Taiwan, of course, is the island nation that constitutes "the other China."

POWER BROKER

TAIWAN RANKS AMONG ONE of the world's most enigmatic countries.

Mountain ranges dominate the eastern two-thirds of the island, which covers an area of nearly 14,000 square miles (35,808 square km). A population of 23.45 million makes Taiwan one of the world's most densely populated countries.

The "Taiwan Miracle" began in the early 1960s, when the island entered a period of rapid economic growth and industrialization. Today, Taiwan ranks an impressive 15th in GDP per capita, buoyed with major contributions from steel, machinery, electronics and chemicals manufacturing.

Taiwan Semiconductor Manufacturing Company, Limited (TSMC) alone makes Taiwan a force to reckon with. It is the world's most valuable semiconductor company and the world's largest dedicated independent semiconductor foundry.

Founded in 1987, TSMC was the world's first dedicated semiconductor foundry and has long been the leading company in its field. In 1997, TSMC became the first Taiwanese company to be listed on the New York Stock Exchange.

With semiconductors now said to be more important than fossil fuels, Taiwan's capital city, Taipei, presides over some valuable turf.

COLONIAL GAMES

So what is the source of the confusion regarding Taiwan's political status?

The start of the story is eerily similar to that of California, another Pacific coastal region whose aboriginal inhabitants came into conflict with European colonial powers. Except Taiwan attracted the attention of the colonial Japanese instead.

Taiwan's location made Chinese stewardship more logical than Japanese or European rule. In 1683, an armada led by Admiral Shi Lang of southern Fujian formally annexed Taiwan for the Qing dynasty.

Taiwan then fell under colonial Japanese rule from 1895 to 1945, when World War II ended.

CIVIL WAR

The end of WWII saw the resumption of the Chinese Civil War. In one corner was the Chinese Nationalists (Kuomintang), led by Chiang Kai-shek. In the other corner was the Chinese Communist Party (CCP), led by CCP Chairman Mao Zedong. The United States actively supported the Nationalists.

In 1949, a series of Communist offensives crushed Nationalist forces on the mainland. However, the nationalist Republic of China (ROC) had one last bargaining chip; Chiang Kai-Shek's supporters simply fled to Taiwan and declared the island the seat of China's true government.

The government-in-exile declared martial law on Taiwan in May 1949; it was only repealed nearly four decades later, in 1987. During the White Terror, as the period became known, some 140,000 people were imprisoned or executed for being perceived as anti-KMT or pro-Communist. Most of the victims represented the intellectual and social elite, resulting in the decimation of an entire generation of political and social leaders.

The U.S. grudgingly abandoned Taiwan to the Communists. However, the Korean War motivated pResident Harry S. Truman to wade in on the side of the Nationalists again. Ironically, the U.S. and United Kingdom couldn't agree on which government rightfully ruled China, leaving Taiwan in political limbo.

NUCLEAR THREATS

The Nationalist retreat to Taiwan wasn't the end of China's civil war. In 1958, Communist Chinese forces began shelling islands controlled by Taiwan in preparation for an invasion of Taiwan. However, the U.S. rushed to Taiwan's defense.

A classified document exposed by Daniel Ellsberg of Pentagon Papers fame reveals that U.S. military leaders even agitated for a nuclear strike against China, which would have hit targets as far north as Shanghai. ("Risk of Nuclear War Over Taiwan in 1958 Said to Be Greater Than Publicly Known," Charlie Savage, *New York Times*, May 22)

U.S. planners thought it was a good idea, even though they assumed that the Soviet Union would aid China and retaliate in kind with nuclear weapons. Such a nuclear shootout would obviously have killed millions.

Faced with the U.S. fleet and the threat of nuclear annihilation, Mao Zedong called off the planned invasion of Taiwan.

But why did Ellsberg disclose this information just recently? Is it simply propaganda designed to convince Chinese leaders that the U.S. is still willing to nuke China today? In other words, is it a lie?

A more likely possibility is that the U.S. government really did consider nuking China, but they kept it secret because news of their evil plot would have tarnished the United States' image. If so, perhaps they decided to make the document public decades later in order to intimidate China's current leaders.

GLOBAL CONSENSUS

After the KMT's retreat to Taiwan, most countries—notably those in the Western Bloc—continued to maintain relations with the ROC. However, recognition gradually eroded, with many countries switching recognition to the People's Republic of China in the 1970's.

Though the ROC was a founding member of the United Nations, it now has neither official membership nor observer status in the organization.

While the People's Republic of China aims for peaceful reunification with Taiwan, it does not rule out the use of force.

On October 25, 1971, UN Resolution 2758 was adopted by 76 votes to 35 with 17 abstentions, recognizing the PRC, founded in 1949 on the mainland, as China's sole representative in the United Nations. Countries in support included France, India, the UK, and the USSR; countries in opposition included Japan and the United States.

The PRC refuses to have diplomatic relations with any nation that has diplomatic relations with the ROC, and it requires all nations with which it has diplomatic relations to make a statement recognizing its claims to Taiwan. As a result, only 13 UN member states and the Holy See maintain official diplomatic relations with the Republic of China (ROC). However, the ROC maintains unofficial relations with most countries via *de facto* embassies and consulates.

The U.S. was a partner with Taiwan in a mutual defense treaty from 1954 to 1979. The U.S. remains one of Taiwan's main supporters and has continued selling arms and providing military training to the Armed Forces through the Taiwan Relations Act passed in 1979.

The People's Republic of China considers U.S. involvement disruptive to the stability of the region.

In January 2010, the U.S. announced its intention to sell $6.4 billion worth of military hardware to Taiwan. As a consequence, the PRC warned that its co-operation with the U.S. on international and regional issues could suffer and that the companies involved—namely Raytheon, Lockheed Martin, Boeing, and United Technologies—could face Chinese sanctions.

The official position of the United States is that the PRC is expected to "use no force or threat[en] to use force against Taiwan" and the ROC is to "exercise prudence in managing all aspects of Cross-Strait relations."

Both are to refrain from performing actions or espousing statements "that would unilaterally alter Taiwan's status."

On December 16, 2015, the Obama administration announced a deal to sell $1.83 billion worth of arms to the armed forces of the ROC. The foreign ministry of the PRC had expressed its disapproval of the sales and issued the U.S. with a "stern warning," saying it would hurt PRC-U.S. relations. In response to U.S. support for Taiwan, the PRC defense minister Wei Fenghe said in 2019 that "If anyone dares to split Taiwan from China, the Chinese military has no choice but to fight at all costs."

About 30,000 US troops were stationed in Taiwan, until the United States established diplomatic relations with the PRC in 1979.

Today, Taiwan maintains a large and technologically advanced military, mainly as a defense against the constant threat of invasion by the People's Liberation Army using the Anti-Secession Law of the People's Republic of China as a pretext. This law authorizes the use of military force when certain conditions are met, such as a danger to mainlanders.

From 1949 to the 1970s, the primary mission of the Taiwanese military was to "retake mainland China" through Project National Glory. As this mission has transitioned away from attack because the relative strength of the PRC has massively increased, the ROC military has begun to shift emphasis from the traditionally dominant army to the air force and navy.

The first line of protection against invasion by the PRC is the ROC's own armed forces. Current ROC military doctrine is to hold out against an invasion or blockade until the U.S. military responds. There is, however, no guarantee in the Taiwan Relations Act or any other treaty that the United States will defend Taiwan, even in the event of invasion.

The joint declaration on security between the U.S. and Japan signed in 1996 may imply that Japan would be involved in any response. However, Japan has refused to stipulate whether the "area surrounding Japan" mentioned in the pact includes Taiwan, and the precise purpose of the pact is unclear. The Australia, New Zealand, United States Security Treaty (ANZUS Treaty) may mean that other U.S. allies, such as Australia, could theoretically be involved. While this would risk damaging economic ties with China, a conflict over

Taiwan could lead to an economic blockade of China by a greater coalition.

THE PERFECT SOLUTION?

I HAVE NO ILL will towards the Taiwanese people. Moreover, I'm an unabashed idealist and humanitarian who likes to see people allowed to live in peace.

With that in mind, allow me to suggest a hopelessly romantic solution to the Taiwan standoff.

Imagine if the People's Republic of China decided to take the high road and allow Taiwan to formally declare itself a sovereign state. Better yet, the two countries become close allies, sharing semiconductor technology and forming a military bulwark against the U.S. and its far flung allies.

China would be far more secure than it is now, and Taiwan would similarly be more secure.

TAIWAN VS HAWAII

To really sweeten the pie, imagine if the U.S. got in on the political love fest. In fact, let's imagine that the U.S. government decided to allow Hawaii to declare itself a sovereign nation belonging to the Hawaiian people. The natives could take back the land appropriated by Crackbook CEO Mark Zuckerberg, and the U.S. military could be given the boot.

Isn't that a wonderful fantasy?

Unfortunately, that kind of idealism seldom sees the light of day.

Taiwan was associated with China long before Hawaii was associated with the U.S. Moreover, Taiwan is quite close to mainland China, while Hawaii is in the middle of the Pacific Ocean. China has a far stronger legal claim to Taiwan than the U.S. has on Hawaii.

But the U.S. government will continue shitting on the Hawaiian people until Hell freezes over, and it will similarly never stop using Taiwan as a wedge against the People's Republic of China.

As for China and Taiwan teaming up on silicon chips, guess again. If China gained control of Taiwan's TSMC, the U.S. would likely view that as an act of war.

In fact, the U.S. exploits Taiwan just as it exploits Japan, the Philippines, India and Australia. All are carefully groomed to impeach China's military security. No matter how nice the Taiwanese people are, the U.S. won't allow them to be anything but mainland China's enemy.

The U.S. is using and exploiting Taiwan, just as it uses and exploits Hawaii.

FOUR TAIWAN CRISES

THERE HAVE BEEN FOUR Taiwan Strait crises—in 1954, 1958, 1995, and 2022—and the trend doesn't look good for Team USA.

1954

After losing a civil war to Mao Zedong's communist forces, Nationalist Party Leader Chiang Kai-shek fled to Taiwan in 1949. Shortly after the end of the Korean War, Beijing tried to deter the Eisenhower administration from signing a mutual defense treaty with Kai-shek.

However, China was unsuccessful; the U.S. and Taiwan signed the defense treaty in 1954.

In the meantime, the U.S. tried to keep Chinese forces from seizing the Taiwanese-held islands of Kinmen and Matsu just off China's southeast coast, though China bombarded the islands with artillery. At the same time, the U.S. wanted to restrain Kai-shek from trying to retake the mainland with a counterattack.

1958

Four years later, there was a second conflict which brought more shelling of the islands. In order to prevent China's takeover of the islands of Kinmen and Matsu, the U.S. military was prepared to use nuclear weapons. Fortunately, pResident Dwight Eisenhower rejected that idea.

Eventually, the two sides adopted a face-saving ritual in which communists and nationalists shelled each other on alternate days, a tradition that continued intermittently for two decades.

1995

The third crisis erupted in 1995 over Taiwanese pResident Lee Teng-hui's visit to his alma mater, Cornell University. Although the Clinton administration initially opposed the idea, it was overruled by a Congressional resolution in support of the visit.

Viewing Lee's visit as yet another betrayal of Washington's commitment to the "one-China policy," China responded with months of military exercises. The show of force was also aimed at deterring Taiwanese voters from voting for Lee in the 1996 presidential election.

However, Beijing's efforts backfired. The U.S. sent two aircraft carrier battle groups to waters near Taiwan, clearly outclassing China's military forces. In addition, Lee was elected with a 54% majority in Taiwan's first-ever direct presidential election.

Susan Shirk, who served as deputy assistant secretary of state in the Bureau of East Asia and Pacific Affairs after the crisis, later suggested that both sides were sobered by how close they had come to a major military encounter. The U.S. and China worked at strengthening their ties, culminating in China's then-president Jiang Zemin making a high-profile visit to the U.S. in 1997.

2022: NANCY PELOSI'S BIG ADVENTURE

Ukrainian pResident (and Jewish comedian) Volodymyr Zelensky made headlines on July 22, 2022 when he and his wife Olena (a former comedy writer) posed for a photoshoot in *Vogue*. (They were photographed by the famous lesbian Jewish photographer Annie Leibovitz.) Earlier, Zelensky hosted American entertainer Ben Stiller, who, like Zelensky, is a Jewish comedian. Still earlier, Zelensky was filmed playing the familiar Jewish folk song "Hava Nagila" with his penis.

Millions of Ukrainians' lives have been upended by war, and thousands of citizens are fighting and dying while Zelensky entertains fellow comedians and poses for fashion magazines. However, another clown quickly stole the limelight from Zelensky, and this clown risked starting World War III far to the east.

CLOWN DIPLOMACY (AKA DUMB AND DUMBER:) IS THERE A CONNECTION BETWEEN PELOSI AND ZELENSKY? (CC—SEE CREDITS)

Of course, you probably know I'm talking about the now famous Nancy Pelosi, a U.S. politician who made a rather extraordinary high-stakes trip to Taiwan, arriving on August 2, 2022.

Pelosi wasn't the first U.S. politician to visit Taiwan, of course. However, her visit was incendiary because she's arguably the third most powerful politician in the U.S. She's the third in the line of pResidential succession. In other words, if the pResident and vice pResident were both killed, Pelosi would become the POTUS ("pResident of the United States" for political novices). As a bonus, she's even older than our senile pResident Joe Biden.

This is how David P. Goldman put it on his Twitter account:

> **"Pelosi is Constitutionally 2nd in line to POTUS, so this is a state visit from the standpoint of diplomatic protocol. That, as a former U.S. UN ambassador told me, is a clear violation of the '72 Shanghai Communique."**

Moreover, Pelosi's timing rubbed salt in the wound.

For starters, relations between the U.S. and China were already sour, thanks to endless lies, provocations, and dirty tricks by the U.S. Second, Pelosi was the first House speaker to travel to Taiwan since Newt Gingrich did so in 1997, a quarter century ago. Is U.S. policy moving backwards? China's government saw the stunt as a threat to its sovereignty.

In addition, Pelosi's visit came ahead of a key congress of the ruling Communist Party later in 2022 at which pResident Xi is expected to obtain a third five-year term as party leader. Xi has made the reunification of Taiwan a core issue. Adding fuel to the fire, some observers claim that China's economy is stumbling, a situation that is allegedly stoking nationalism.

SNEAKY WITCH

Pelosi didn't make an open, dignified diplomatic journey to Taiwan. She could more accurately be described as a thief in the night, a shifty-eyed burglar cunningly searching for an entrance into someone's home.

In fact, Pelosi had planned to lead a congressional delegation to Taiwan in early April. When China's government began blasting Pelosi, she apparently had second thoughts ("China Rips Pelosi Over Reported Taiwan Trip, Setting Up Showdown," Bloomberg News, April 7, 2022). But how could she cancel the trip without appearing weak?

Simple. Pelosi simply announced she had COVID ("Pelosi tests positive for coronavirus as part of D.C. wave of cases," Amy B. Wang, Paul Kane and Tyler Pager, *Washington Post*, April 7, 2022). The precise timing of Pelosi's diagnosis was utterly unbelievable; she lied about having COVID so she would have an excuse to chicken out of her Taiwan junket.

However, Pelosi wasn't finished. During the summer, she once again announced her intention of making a diplomatic trip to Taiwan. China once again responded with rage.

This time, the media reported that pResident Joe Biden hadn't approved Pelosi's trip, and the U.S. military advised against it. They sent out the message that Pelosi had dropped Taiwan from her itinerary. She would simply visit some other Asian countries.

And so the world was stunned when the headlines suddenly announced that Pelosi was in Taiwan! However, Pelosi didn't visit Taiwan like a respectable dignitary. Rather, she scrapped the relatively direct path from Kuala Lumpur, Malaysia to Taiwan in favor of a three-hour detour around Borneo and the Philippines in an apparent effort to avoid the South China Sea, where China had built up a military presence ("Why Pelosi's flight to Taiwan took a three-hour detour," Ryan King, *Washington Examiner*, Aug. 2, 2022).

CORPORATE WHORES

As we will soon learn, Nancy Pelosi, who is one of the richest members of Congress (itself a millionaires' club), uses her office to enrich herself. Her involvement in the destruction of Libya makes her a de facto war criminal.

For good measure, her husband, Paul, is one helluva asshole, too.

On May 28, 2022, he was driving while intoxicated when he slammed his Porsche into another car, reportedly injuring the driver ("Nancy Pelosi's husband, Paul, pleads not guilty over DUI crash," Marjorie Hernandez and Emily Crane, *New York Post*, Aug. 3, 2022). All that was missing was Volodymyr Zelensky and his *Vogue* photographer.

Pelosi was reportedly found in his damaged car near the intersection of California Route 29 and Oakville Cross Road. He "reportedly gave the responding officers his California Highway Patrol 11-99 (CHP 11-99) Foundation — a pro-police charity — membership card when pulled over" ("Paul Pelosi charges: watchdogs warn against 'special treatment' in DUI case," Houston Keene, Fox News).

Mr. Pelosi was reportedly arraigned on a pair of misdemeanor charges in a case that typically begins with a felony booking, more evidence of the double standard that slithers through the "D.C. Swamp."

It wasn't Pelosi's first car accident. He had another accident in 1957, in which his older brother died ("Nancy Pelosi's husband killed his older brother in 1957 sports car crash: report," Emily Crane, *New York Post*, May 31, 2022). Pelosi, who was then a minor, was exonerated of misdemeanor manslaughter charges.

Nor was Nancy Pelosi's Taiwan excursion her first exercise in China bashing.

In 1991, Pelosi visited China's famous Tianamen Square with two other corrupt politicians, U.S. Representatives Ben Jones and John Miller. There, they unfurled a banner that proclaimed, "To those who died for democracy in China."

More recently, Pelosi gained notoriety for a comment she made on political events in Hong Kong: "a beautiful sight to behold."

Critics said she was gloating over the violent riots that shattered Hong Kong. Supporters countered that her comment was taken out of context; she was actually commenting on a peaceful candlelight vigil staged in memory of the Beijing demonstrators who lost their lives in the Tiananmen demonstrations on June 4, 1989.

However, one has to wonder if the details really matter. This is the same twisted bitch who gloated over the destruction of Libya.

Why does she care about democracy in China but not in Libya? Why does she care more about oppressed Chinese than Native Americans?

This empress has no clothes.

Nancy and Paul Pelosi aren't fine, upstanding citizens, They aren't real Americans. They don't give a rat's ass about democracy. They don't care about the little people, and they don't represent us. Hell, they haven't even learned how to drive! They are de facto traitors.

Maybe they should co-author a book, *Stock Tips* for WWIII.

WHY?

So, why did Nancy Pelosi make such a reckless move, and who benefited from it?

At first glance, it would appear that Pelosi was simply flexing Team USA's muscles, assuring the Taiwanese that they would not share Ukraine's fate. Team USA said "we're visiting Taiwan," China countered "No you aren't," and the U.S. carried out its threat. The U.S. thus appeared to come out the winner, but take a closer look.

Pelosi promoted her trip to Taiwan as a blow for democracy. She had earlier clinched her title as a champion of democracy when she joined Hillary Clinton in gloating over the murder of Libyan leader

Muammar Gaddafi (Press Release: "Pelosi Statement on Libya," Oct. 20, 2011):

> "Today's news marks the next phase of Libya's march toward democracy. After decades of tyrannical rule in Libya, the world is hopeful that the next generation of Libyan leaders will bring their country out of this dark chapter. The strong action taken by the United States, led by pResident Obama, and NATO, the United Nations and the Arab League proves the power of the world community working together.

> "The United States has and will continue to work with the Libyan people to achieve their aspirations for freedom, a democratic government and the rule of law."

As you may know (if you've done your homework), Libya boasted the highest standard of living of any African country until pResident Obama spearheaded its invasion and destruction by NATO, turning it into a borderline failed state. And, no, Gaddafi wasn't a tyrant. Operation Libyan Democracy was a stunningly tragic failure, to put it politely.

Some reports suggested that Pelosi's real reason for visiting Taiwan was more personal. She knew the Democrats were going to get hosed in the mid-term elections, so she wanted to boost her political résumé with a tough-on-China image.

Or maybe Pelosi simply wanted to boost her financial fortune. A rich bitch, she was already worth over $100 million, much of it earned from investing in sleazy corporations like Microsoft and Google.

Not surprisingly, Ms. Democracy opposes increasing regulations on stock trades by members of Congress, stating that "We're a free market economy" and congresspeople "should be able to participate in that." Her statement was even criticized by fellow Democrats who favor banning stock trades by members of Congress.

Maybe the answer is "Hurricane Pelosi careened into Taiwan for all the above reasons."

It is doubtful that Pelosi could or would have made her reckless trip without approval from the entities that control the U.S. government. They presumably wanted to flex America's muscles, and if Pelosi could also boost her image and rake in a little more money at the same time, why not?

In this spirit, the comments about Joe Biden not approving of Pelosi's mission are meaningless, because Joe Biden isn't in charge. Even if he was in charge, he could easily tell the media he didn't approve of Pelosi's trip when he really did.

During the 1995 Taiwan crisis, the Clinton administration squared off against Congress, which passed a resolution supporting Taiwanese pResident Lee Teng-hui's visit to Cornell University. If pResident Biden was seriously opposed to Pelosi's trip, couldn't he have pressured Congress into passing a similar resolution? Instead, Sneaky Joe just gave lip service to opposing the trip.

FALLOUT

Whether Pelosi's blitzkrieg back-door blow for democracy was really a victory for the U.S. is hard to say.

Is Taiwan's security now better? It might actually be worse.

Are U.S.-China relations better? They're clearly worse. China surrounded Taiwan with military forces before launching a series of high profile military drills.

Amazingly, Pelosi's visit may have even alienated many Taiwanese. In fact, a majority of Taiwanese were angered by her visit, according to one survey. Protesters carried signs that demanded "Ugly American witch go home."

JUST TWO DAYS AFTER NANCY PELOSI TOUCHED DOWN IN TAIWAN, THREE PEOPLE WERE KILLED BY A LIGHTNING STRIKE ACROSS THE STREET FROM THE WHITE HOUSE. IT PROBABLY WASN'T THE RESULT OF SOME TOP SECRET CHINESE SECRET WEAPON, BUT IT DOES SERVE AS A REMINDER THAT WHAT GOES AROUND COMES AROUND.

In "Nancy Pelosi, You Silly Biddy," (*Eurasia Review*, Aug. 4, 2022), Binoy Kampmark compared Pelosi's trip to Archduke Franz Ferdinand's spectacularly foolish 1914 visit to Sarajevo, which sparked World War I. (No, the Germans didn't start WWI, or even WWII for that matter.)

In the final analysis, what U.S. politicians and media whores describe as a blow for democracy looks very different in the eyes of millions of people around the world. They see an arrogant, aging free market whore who may be as senile as pResident Joe Biden, an American witch who tricked her way into Taiwan, callously risking World War III over her personal agenda, an agenda that ironically alienated many, if not most, Taiwanese.

South Korea's president declined to meet with Pelosi when she visited his country, apparently in a move to placate China, which is South Korea's biggest trading partner. While Pelosi's wayward husband drank a cup of hot coffee, the media were reporting economic fallout due to his wife's wayward errand. The headlines say it all.

"Nancy Pelosi's Taiwan trip sends stocks tumbling," Laura He, CNN, Aug. 2, 2022

"Chip stocks plunge as Nancy Pelosi lands in Taiwan. Here's why the chip sector in particular could lose big if China follows through on its threat of 'strong countermeasures,'" Yvonne Lau, The Guardian, Aug. 2, 2022

Pelosi's big adventure had all the planning and tact of a bull in a china shop (pun intended). Or maybe we should make that a *bull-shitter* in a China shop, as Nancy "Blabbermouth Express" Pelosi's jet spread a trail of democracy vapor across Asia.

Xi Jinping has stated that Taiwan will be reunited with China by 2049, which is actually an awfully long ways away. As China's power increases and America's goes downhill, that deadline increasingly looks like 2030. And with arrogant U.S. politicians and media whores continuously provoking China, it's possible it could even happen sooner.

When China does make its move, all eyes will be on the U.S. Wouldn't it be funny if the U.S. declared war, only to discover that it has been abandoned by allies who are sickened by its never-ending self-serving games? While the media chant "Remember the Alamo," former allies might counter "Remember Nancy Pelosi!" or "Remember Libya!"

■ ■

In summary, Nancy Pelosi might be considered a modern-day Benedict Arnold. On the other hand, Arnold may have actually been a pretty honorable guy who had some good reasons for switching sides. Pelosi, of course, hasn't really switched sides at all. She's still working for the same power brokers she has always shilled for. Screw the American people, and screw the world.

TAIWAN CRISIS V

So, if we examine the four Taiwan crises, can we discern any trends that might help us predict the nature and outcome of the next crisis?

For starters, the military calculus has changed. American right-wingers can still boast about nuking China, but China can nuke the U.S. right back. China's conventional forces are also much more powerful. Many authorities openly question whether the U.S. would prevail in a war against China. Even if the U.S. won, it could be a very costly victory, possibly a Pyrrhic victory.

At the same time, China is more committed to reunification than ever before, while the U.S. is more committed to playing games. One of Xi Jinping's key goals is the rejuvenation of the Chinese nation, making him more personally attached to Taiwan policy than previous leaders.

In contrast, the U.S. is more firmly committed to talking out of both sides of its lying face, with corrupt politicians like Nancy Pelosi sneaking into Taiwan and taking potshots at China before fleeing the scene of the crime.

At the same time, there has been a change in global attitudes, with virtually no country recognizing Taiwan as a sovereign nation. Combined with a growing contempt for the U.S.—the ally that shits on its allies—we have a recipe for a Chinese takeover of Taiwan.

The next Taiwan crisis could easily be the last, and whether it ends in World War III is up to the U.S.

In the meantime, I'd like to see a new comedy sitcom starring Nancy Pelosi and Volodowhore Zelensky, with lots of nude photos of Nancy in a smashed Porsche. What would be a good title—*War Whores, Which Way to the Front?, Ukraine to Taiwan, With Friends Like These, My Favorite Allies, Club Democracy*? Or maybe we could combine "Pelosi" and "Zelensky" to form the portmanteau *Polanski*.

DIAOYUTAI ISLANDS

The Diaoyutai Islands are a group of uninhabited islands in the western North Pacific. Their political status is evidenced by their variety of names, including Senkaku Islands.

So who is the rightful owner of these islands?

The islands are much closer to mainland China than they are to Japan, and they are closer still to Taiwan.

Moreover, China claims the discovery and ownership of the islands from the 14th century, while Japan's ownership lasted from 1895 until its surrender at the end of World War II. The U.S. then took control, administering the islands from 1945-1972, when they were returned to Japanese control under the Okinawa Reversion Agreement.

So the imperialistic U.S. and Japan get to control islands near mainland China that were part of the Chinese empire in the 14th century?

Today, China and Japan are feuding over the islands.

I would obviously like to see these islands returned to China. An alternative option would be to designate the islands a biological reserve belonging to no nation. That might be an option favored by the islands' best-known resident, the short-tailed albatross.

The saga of China's role in the South China Sea is complex. Unlike Hong Kong, Taiwan and Tibet, the vast region was not historically part of the Chinese empire.

China's government has simply appointed itself guardian of the South China Sea. In the process, China has thumbed its nose at other country's territorial claims, engaged in illegal fishing, and militarized portions of the South China Sea.

So why would China court world opinion with such bad behavior?

The South China Sea is a region of tremendous economic and geostrategic importance. It is the second most used sea lane in the world. Huge oil and natural gas reserves are believed to lie beneath its seabed. The South China Sea's rich fisheries are coveted by the millions of people who live in Southeast Asia, along with China.

National security could also be an issue.

China has long been vulnerable to exploitation by Western powers. The Great Wall of China offered some protection from Central Asian nomads, but how do you build a great wall across the sea?

As China's economy grows in power, unfettered access to important sea routes will only become more important. Is China's government worried that the U.S. Navy will play games with Chinese commerce, particularly its Belt and Road initiative?

The U.S. has recruited allies stretching from Europe to Australia, India and Japan. Together, they have sent an armada to patrol the South China Sea. So what's the verdict: Are they merely enforcing the law of the sea, or are they trying to stir up trouble?

How would the U.S. react if China sent a fleet of ships to patrol the Caribbean?

If China is a bad actor that needs to be held accountable by an international tribunal, it's hardly alone. Taiwan also claims the South China Sea for itself.

The Philippines and several countries in Southeast Asia have competing claims over various island archipelagos in the South China Sea. Fish stocks in the region are already heavily depleted. Indonesian authorities have seized and sunk fishing boats belonging to Vietnam and the Philippines.

In fact, Vietnam-flagged vessels are the most frequent illegal fishers in the South China Sea, which is hardly surprising when it has the largest fishing fleet operating in the region—nearly 130,000 vessels compared to 92,300 for China.

Vietnamese critics may be correct to accuse China of violating the UN Convention on the Law of the Sea (UNCLOS), building on and militarizing low-tide features, using its maritime militia to engage in intimidation, and allowing illegal fishing in other countries' exclusive economic zones. The irony is that Vietnam is guilty of all the above as well.

Ultimately, there are no angels in the South China Sea, which is a classic example of the tragedy of the commons, where a beautiful, diverse portion of the planet is raped by all its neighbors in the absence of a universal law or spirit of protection.

The best we can hope for is that the various countries bordering the South China Sea can one day hammer out an agreement, especially one that protects the environment.

As a bonus, I would like to see Western warships banned from the area. The commercial shipping that plows through the South China Sea on a daily basis takes a big enough toll on the environment.

PERSONAL RESPONSIBILITY

While the U.S. has acquired a reputation as a nation of trailer park trash, China has a much cleaner image.

Of course, it depends on who you talk to. Western media whores like to describe the U.S. as a beacon of democracy and human rights while demonizing China as an authoritarian labor camp.

Having lived, taught, worked and engaged in political activism in liberal Seattle, I beg to differ. Seattle is a West Coast sewer crawling with shallow yuppies, trailer park trash and homeless people. I don't know exactly how China compares, but I suspect it's significantly better in many respects.

China has been much more aggressive in fighting poverty, and its infrastructure is an embarrassment to the U.S.

If you check out Wikipedia's article "List of countries by incarceration rate," you will see that there are nearly 2,100,000 people incarcerated in the U.S., more than any other country in the world. China is ranked a fairly close second place, with 1,710,000 incarcerated.

But remember, China has a vastly bigger population than the U.S. If we focus on the per capita incarceration rate, the U.S. remains in first place, but China drops to #129.

So what does it mean? Are Chinese citizens generally more law abiding? Or does its supposedly authoritarian government just not hold criminals accountable?

One class of citizens who appear to have a hard time dodging accountability is China's billionaires.

That's right, there are more billionaires in "communist" China—616 in 2021—than any other country but the U.S., with 724. If we adjust for population, the U.S. still has a lot more billionaires per capita, a reminder that it is the land of capitalist corruption.

But the interesting thing about China's billionaires is the fact that they are so often in the news as targets of government discipline. They sometimes incur the government's wrath because of tax evasion, though Chinese billionaires also have to be careful about what they say about the government.

So what do you think, is this an example of deranged authoritarianism, or is it a welcome change from the U.S., where billionaires effectively own the government (and the country)?

U.S. corporate tycoons are clearly concerned; media whores commonly warn about China's authoritarian government taking a wrecking ball to creativity or entrepreneurship. Clearly, they want to see those billionaires left alone.

A number of popular Chinese celebrities have similarly been nailed for tax evasion.

But it isn't just about money. Chinese authorities have also been waging war on what they see as unhealthy or immoral elements within the entertainment and cultural industries. Prominent business leaders are similarly held to high moral standards.

According to state media reports, Chinese celebs have been warned that they must ensure they "consciously abandon vulgar and kitsch inferior tastes, and consciously oppose the decadent ideas of money worship, hedonism, and extreme individualism."

The tech industry has faced waves of regulatory changes and investigations. Celebrity fandom is seen as a vice, and online gaming has been strictly curtailed, in the name of protecting children.

Now we're in treacherous waters. Is it OK for government to legislate morality?

And what's wrong with extreme individualism? I don't think I've ever met anyone more individualistic than myself. Most of my biggest heroes are pretty extreme individuals.

And so this is a Chinese policy that I'm not completely comfortable with. However, when I look at the wretched filth that engulfs American society, I'm tempted to scream "Viva China!"

Imagine if Bill Gates, Jeffrey Epstein, Jeff Bezos, Elon Musk, Woody Allen and Harvey Weinstein were all Chinese citizens. Would China's government allow them to get away with their crimes? Would Chinese citizens be allowed to peddle pedophilia, either in movies or in real life?

A similar issue is China's penchant for banning U.S. websites. Sites that are banned under China's "Great Firewall" include Google, YouTube, Facebook, Twitter, Wikipedia and Quora.

Frankly, I wish these sites were all banned in the U.S., but *why* are they banned in China? (Hypocrisy alert: Yes, I regularly use some of these sites myself. However, ... well, let's just say it's complicated.)

Are they feared as foreign competition? Or are Chinese authorities just afraid of the propaganda that infests these sites? But who decides what constitutes propaganda to begin with?

To be perfectly honest, I can't identify all the propaganda in Wikipedia or the social networks myself. But there's no question that these sites reek of propaganda and surveillance.

This appears to be a classic study in political philosophy. We're dealing with a witches' brew of complex issues, and it would be virtually impossible for any government to come up with a perfect solution.

Personally, I think China's government is doing a much better job than the U.S. government. As I said, I've seen too much trailer park trash in my country. I've seen the crappy public schools children attend in liberal Seattle. I've been spammed and banned from Facebook and other social networks more times than I can count, all for speaking the truth.

Perhaps morality cannot and should not be legislated, but that doesn't mean we can't make some effort to rein in immorality.

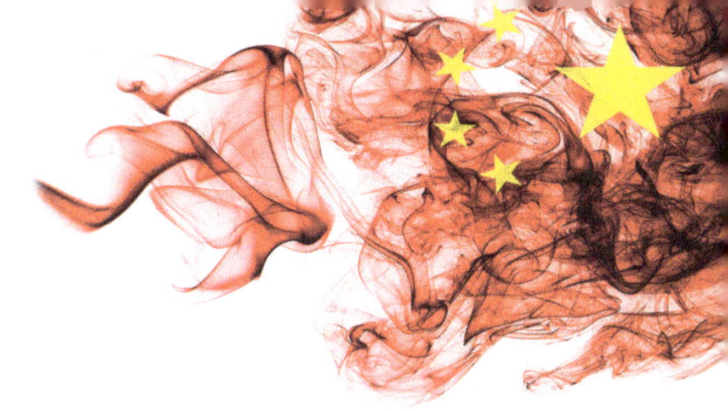

INTERNATIONAL AFFAIRS

Compared to the U.S., China's military might actually be considered a domestic issue, but China's economy and technological prowess are reshaping the world.

ECONOMY

If money is the root of all evil, then China should be eyed with suspicion. How can Chinese communism be more ethical than U.S. capitalism, when both countries are addicted to corporate profits?

On the one hand, I would argue that no country that pursues economic supremacy with China's zeal could be a candidate for sainthood.

On the other hand, is it possible to succeed at commerce without selling your soul to the devil? Even if you can't be perfect, can you not be better than your rival?

If that rival is the U.S., the answer is a resounding YES.

The U.S. is simply a global scumbag. It lies, cheats and steals as it screws its own citizens as viciously as it screws people in other countries. There is no honor among Wall Street bankers and corporate tycoons.

As China increasingly competes for business in countries around the world, it appears to be operating on a higher plane. I will never forgive China for its dam-building spree, but I don't see China screwing people in Latin America and Africa the way they are screwed by the U.S.

Another remarkable thing: China is on the verge of overtaking the U.S. as the world's most powerful country without firing a shot. Merely making a better cell phone, the legendary Huawei, helped. Buying a Huawei and realizing how much more secure I felt without a mobile device cluttered with Google spyware helped make me a fan of China.

When given the choice between buying something made in the U.S. versus something made in China, I will definitely consider the latter. Having upgraded from a Windows PC to a Mac years ago, I'm now looking forward to the day I can upgrade to a Chinese laptop powered by carbon-based chips and a Chinese operating system.

I can't wait until China's digital currency comes online. Would it be possible for a U.S. citizen to ditch his U.S. bank accounts and manage his financial affairs with Chinese assets? Frankly, I'm sick of being screwed by U.S. banksters with their goddam bailouts.

On the negative side, the day may come when Americans are little more than colonial slaves of China. But how is that any worse than being a slave to Bill Gates and his genetically modified food empire? Perhaps we'll discover that the Chinese actually treat us better than our own government does.

Some are predicting that China's economy will overtake the U.S. by 2028. Others are saying it will never happen. And then there are those who say China will technically overtake the U.S., but the U.S. will remain richer for half a century.

Time will tell, of course. However, I see China as a moving target that's going to be awfully hard to stop. At the same time, the U.S. is a bad joke that will be increasingly hard to keep on its feet.

The super rich people who own America may remain rich for half a century, but the prospects for the average U.S. citizen are bleak. China could find itself ruling a two-class colony.

If China can dominate the emerging carbon-chip industry, watch out. That feat alone could pump trillions of dollars into its economy. Could it happen by 2030?

Of course, it takes a strong economy to develop and maintain a strong military. Although I'm no big fan of militarization, I recognize it as a necessary evil. If China's military can keep my country's military bottled up, then God bless China.

After China turns the U.S. into a commercial colony, Americans might finally open their eyes and realize how savagely they've been betrayed by their own leaders. Maybe Americans will one day revolt and topple their own government. Imagine if they used nifty weapons manufactured in China to do the job.

POPULAR COMPLAINTS

FROM JOB THEFT TO intellectual property theft, hazardous products to hazardous sweatshops, Americans have plenty to complain about when it comes to China. The funny thing is that some of these problems are worse in the U.S.

TAKING OUR JOBS

On June 25, 1867, thousands of Chinese railroad workers staged a strike. This was long before China was criss-crossed by bullet trains. These workers were building railroads in the western U.S. They wanted equal pay to white laborers, shorter workdays, and better conditions. The strike ended after the Central Pacific Railroad director shut off their food supply.

There probably weren't many complaints about the Chinese railroad workers taking jobs from white people, because they were doing a job that few whites could stomach. But after the railroad tracks were laid, there would be complaints about Chinamen taking Americans' jobs, which led to the 1882 Chinese Exclusion Act.

Two centuries later, millions of Americans started complaining about losing not just their jobs but entire industries to Chinese citizens residing in China.

THE PRESENCE OF STARBUCKS AND WESTERN FAST FOOD CHAINS IN CHINA IS A REMINDER THAT WE'RE TAKING THEIR JOBS, TOO.

To clarify things, it should be pointed out that U.S. jobs were "outsourced" to China by corporate tycoons, the same privileged bastards who are now trash-talking China. So if you want to blame the Chinese for downsizing American labor, don't forget to thank the back-stabbing assholes we all work for.

Looking at it from another perspective, some have argued that the real villain is technology. Thanks to technology, one person can now do what once took two, half a dozen or 50 people to do years ago, depending on the occupation. Automation and artificial intelligence are making the situation even worse. Every automated checkout machine in a grocery store probably represents one individual who was forced to look for a new job.

Yet many Americans are more likely to complain about Chinese citizens than outsourcing or technology. God forbid that we criticize St. Bill Gates for persuading Congress to change the rules so he could import an army of Indians to take high-paying jobs that could have gone to U.S. citizens.

INTELLECTUAL PROPERTY THEFT

China is widely criticized as a bastion of intellectual property (IP) theft.

The charges are probably true to an extent, but how is China any different from the U.S.?

BILL GATES IS WIDELY ACCUSED OF STEALING OTHER PEOPLE'S IDEAS.

In fact, U.S. corporations are notorious for spying on competitors around the word. They may also be closely tied to the government, which does their spying for them. Google has an office in the Pentagon, for example.

Another problem commonly encountered in the West is the filing of frivolous patents, which is somewhat similar to the filing of patents on things that have already been invented.

Crappy patents are in turn somewhat related to "patent trolls"— entities that buy up patents, then engage in blackmail, threatening to sue companies they claim are infringing on their patents. Many people find it cheaper to pay the trolls what they want rather than go to court.

Perhaps the most odious of patent trolls is Washington State's Intellectual Ventures, which has acquired 95,000 patents or more. Famous for hiding behind thousands of shell companies, the company is headed by Nathan Myhrvold, who formerly served as Microsoft's chief technology officer. (See "When Patents Attack," NPR, July 22, 2011)

In 2015, patent litigation increased 13 percent from the previous year, and two thirds of the suits were brought by patent trolls, doubtless including Nathan Myhrvold.

Such practices stifle innovation, which may be one reason the U.S. is having a hard time competing with Chinese creativity. After all, the high-tech scene in the U.S. has long been dominated by Microsoft, Apple and Google.

All of the above beg the question: *Is it fair to expect China to submit to the U.S. patent system?*

That may not be an option; in 2009, Intellectual Ventures expanded into several other countries, including China. Is it a global fungus?

It would be interesting to know which country is working harder to clean up its act, the U.S. or China. I'd wager there are far more skeletons in America' closet.

GOVERNMENT SUBSIDIES

Western politicians and media whores constantly whine about China's government and corporate sector being joined at the hip. Corporations are supposedly subsidized by the government, which they feed intelligence in return.

Hasn't this long been business as usual in the U.S.?

Where would Bill Gates be without corporate welfare?

Boeing raked in so much money from obscene tax breaks it ran afoul of the World Trade Organization, prompting Boeing to frantically attempt to give some of the money back.

Is that funny or what?

I mentioned that Google has an office in the Pentagon. Speaking of which, it's no secret that the U.S. government spies on both U.S. citizens and people around the world.

Whose technology do you suppose they use in their massive surveillance campaign?

And how many government-employed or sponsored propagandists do you suppose post on Facebook?

Didn't you just love those enormous bailouts bankers got while millions of Americans were losing their jobs and homes after pResident George W. Bush and the bankers themselves crashed the economy?

Personally, I hope China's corporations are working hand-in-hand with their government. As they say, if you can't beat 'em, join 'em.

HAZARDOUS PRODUCTS

In *Fearing China*, Terry D. Wittenmyer says the largest toy recall in 2007 was for 18.5 million toys that were stamped "Made in China." U.S. media whores obligingly churned out headlines blasting the evil Chinese for endangering America's children.

The catch? The problem with the toys lay in the design, not the manufacturing process. Moreover, they were designed by an American company, Mattel. In fact, there are plenty of hazardous products right here in America. Like the lead pipes in Seattle's public schools that officials were mysteriously slow to act on.

Lest you think China's government is too soft on people who endanger citizens' health, consider Zheng Xiaoyu, the former director of China's State Food and Drug Administration. He was executed in 2007 for taking bribes in exchange for approving untested medicine.

IF THE SACKLERS LIVED IN CHINA, THEY PROBABLY WOULD HAVE BEEN EXECUTED LONG AGO.

Imagine if George W. Bush received a death sentence. Most U.S. citizens would probably think that would be excessive, but would it really be so bad? How about that mega-quack Bill Gates? How about the Sackler family of opioid fame, whose business has killed countless thousands of people?

In the meantime, China has experienced a dramatic increase in diabetes, fueled by an explosion of Western fast food franchises. Fortunately, China's rate of diabetes is still lower than that of the U.S., which leads developed nations in diabetes prevalence.

SLAVE LABOR

It is popularly claimed that China cranks out cheap products with the help of sweatshops and substandard labor laws. At the very least, Chinese workers work long hours and are paid low wages.

DUH...isn't that why U.S. corporations outsourced so many jobs to China in the first place? And if we're going to criticize a company that treats workers poorly, shouldn't we also criticize the U.S. teenager who buys five pairs of tennis shoes manufactured by that company?

Bear in mind that the Chinese aren't as pampered as Americans. Many of the people working in China's urban sweatshops left even more grueling, lower-paying jobs in rural areas. As China' economy continues to grow, working conditions and pay will improve. It's the same script the U.S. followed.

In the meantime, Microsoft propagandists like to complain about Apple laptops and iPhones being produced in Chinese sweatshops where desperately unhappy workers commit suicide. If the stories are true, then we should certainly hope the Chinese will clean up their act. But doesn't Microsoft's crappy software require hardware, too? Even if the hardware isn't owned by Microsoft, there's still a clear link.

So what conditions are PCs manufactured under?

Fortunately, computers aren't manufactured in the Common-wealth of the Northern Marianas Islands (CNMI), as far as I know. The islands are better known for clothing made in foreign-owned sweatshops. Yet there's still a Microsoft connection.

The CNMI is a U.S. commonwealth, a status that allows it to slap a "Made in USA" label on goods manufactured on Saipan. But does Saipan represent the values U.S. politicians claim *they* represent?

Some 91% of the local workforce consists of immigrants (many of them Chinese) who are being paid barely half the U.S. minimum hourly wage. Stories have emerged of workers forced to live behind barbed wire in squalid shacks without plumbing. It gets worse.

A Department of the Interior report found that "Chinese women were subject to forced abortions and that women and children were subject to forced prostitution in the local sex-tourism industry."

In response, the U.S. Senate unanimously passed a worker reform bill, but it was blocked by Tom DeLay in the House.

In 1993, the government of the CNMI hired Preston Gates to lobby for it. The "Gates" stands for Bill Gates's creepy father. (The law firm was later renamed K&L Gates.) The CNMI government was one of the law firm's biggest clients, paying it about $6.7 million between 1993 and 2001.

A sleazy lobbyist named Jack Abramoff took on the Northern Mariana Islands (CNMI) as a client in 1995, the year I had my political awakening. He was employed by Preston Gates.

Abramoff's lobbying team helped Rep. Ralph Hall (R-TX) to craft statements attacking the credibility of "Katrina," a teenaged sex slave whom federal officials relocated to Hawaii and who testified to federal investigators and Congress about Saipan's sex trade, in the process forestalling a federal criminal prosecution. There's much more to the story, but I won't relate it all here.

Amazingly, Abramoff eventually paid for his crimes—sort of. He was one of 24 people convicted of a wide variety of crimes in 2006.

In 2008, Abramoff was sentenced to a four-year prison term, to be served concurrently with previous sentences. He ultimately served four years of a six-year sentence.

After his release, Abramoff wrote the autobiographical book *Capitol Punishment: The Hard Truth About Washington Corruption From America's Most Notorious Lobbyist*. He doubtless used his campaign against corruption in the lobbying industry to promote his book.

In 2020, it was reported that Abramoff was headed back to jail. The stupid bastard was the first person to be charged with flouting the Lobbying Disclosure Act, which was amended in 2007 after details of his earlier scheme(s) emerged.

It's nice to know that Abramoff has been given a taste of accountability. But were Abramoff, Tom DeLay or any of their cronies ever held accountable for effectively aiding and abetting sex trafficking in the Marianas back in the 1990's? What was the fate of the women and children who were among the victims?

None of this should detract from any similar crimes that might have occurred in China. But before you start throwing rocks, you might want to take a look in a mirror.

In the meantime, what about working conditions in the U.S.? What about the countless people working without benefits? What about families in which both spouses work two or three jobs in order to pay the rent and feed the kids?

I was a victim of some pretty extraordinary tyranny when I worked as a teacher for the Seattle School District. Ditto when I worked for the U.S. Postal Service. After I went to work for UPS, I had a derelict supervisor who turned out to be an ex-cop who was a serial rapist and a double murder suspect.

So don't lecture me about working conditions in China. At the very least, they will probably continue improving along with China's rapidly growing economy.

YUAN VS DOLLAR

What force of Nature is more powerful than the U.S. dollar? For generations, the dollar has financed and won wars. It has bullied other countries into submission and financed their exploitation by capitalist thugs curled up in the bowels of New York City.

Other units of currency have challenged the U.S. dollar, but none has ever toppled it. At last, that could change.

Its status as the world's second biggest economy gives China's official currency, the renminbi, default bragging rights. The basic unit of the renminbi is the yuan, a word that is also used to refer to Chinese currency in general, especially in international contexts.

Countries that rank as unofficial users of the yuan are currently just about limited to Macau, Laos, North Korea, Myanmar, Nepal, Venezuela and Zimbabwe. However, the list will probably grow soon enough.

INTERNATIONAL BANKING

CHINA IS ALREADY MAKING its financial clout felt in the realm of international banking, a domain long ruled by New York City's "banksters," notably operating through the International Monetary Fund (IMF) and World Bank.

Countries have long been pressured into borrowing exorbitant sums of money from the IMF and World Bank. If they don't want to borrow, they can be persuaded. Assassinations and political coups can be engineered, and the new, corrupt governments may be only too willing to borrow beyond their countries' means of paying the tab.

In addition, borrowing money from the IMF and World Bank typically obligates debtor governments to implement draconian policies dictated by banksters. Workers might see their pensions shredded, while education is short-changed. Entire societies are regularly devastated for the profits of a mob of fat cats holed up in New York City.

Today, needy governments can choose between borrowing from New York City or China.

Media whores sometimes moan about China setting up "debt traps" that force debtor countries that can't pay their debts to hand over valuable assets instead. However, those stories appear to be few and far in between and seldom pan out to boot. Even if such stories were true, countries would still be able to choose their poison: China or New York City.

Today, many countries are doing business with China, and that often appears to be a win-win situation.

DIGITAL CURRENCY

IN THE MEANTIME, THE U.S. dollar is bracing for what could be an even bigger blow in the form of digital currency. In particular, think about an electronic Chinese yuan (e-CNY).

The U.S. reaction is perfectly predictable. In "China's Digital Yuan: A Threat to Freedom" (August 25, 2021), James Dorn of the right-wing Cato Institute argued that

> **"The dollar has earned its status as a safe-haven currency because it is backed by trust in U.S. institutions that safeguard basic freedoms and private property rights."**

Dorn adds that global traders lack confidence in "China's adherence to the norms of civil society and the rule of law," adding that "China lacks those institutions and trust."

As a U.S. citizen, political activist and student of politics, I have no trust in U.S. institutions whatsoever. My parents lived through the Great Depression, and I recall the horror and mayhem when George W. Bush and the bankers crashed the economy. My basic freedoms are under growing assault, and who can afford private property these days anyway?

And how does the U.S. out-shine China in terms of adherence to the norms of civil society and the rule of law?

China has done far more to fight poverty on its own soil than the U.S. has. Nor is China following the United States' lead in sowing poverty in other countries. Where was the United States' respect for the rule of law when it invaded Afghanistan, Iraq, Syria and Libya and declared sanctions against Iran, Venezuela and Cuba?

And so I cheer for China's digital currency and pray it vanquishes the U.S. dollar.

In the meantime, some Chinese officials are calling for the renminbi to serve as Southeast Asia's regional currency. From there, it would be a short step to a digital Southeast Asian currency, something the U.S. would not be too excited about.

TECHNOLOGY

When it comes to technology, the Chinese don't mess around. They have an army of top-notch scientists and a can-do attitude that makes them dangerous competitors.

I say "dangerous" because you really don't want to be forced to compete with them. It's much better to cooperate with the Chinese, as they appear to be far more cooperative than Americans, who prefer competition.

Like that stupid asshole of a pResident Donald Trump, who started a trade war with China then nearly went ballistic in trashing Huawei. Or that stupid asshole of a successor Joe Biden, a senile nitwit who is continuing Trump's policies.

The silicon chip shortage and supply chain problems can probably both be blamed on Team USA's insane war against China. The ultimate irony is the fact that we're probably destined to lose.

The U.S. government's silicon chip strategy is causing China a lot of pain in the short run, but it has also motivated China to seek independence in that arena. In fact, the normally cooperative Chinese are probably going to become more independent in many arenas.

I could be wrong; maybe China will crash and burn. But I suspect the Chinese will make some big gains in 2022. By 2025, Donald

Trump will probably be pissing his pants. (Hopefully, Biden will be dead by then.)

CYBERATTACKS

WHILE ADOLF HITLER WASN'T able to draw blood on U.S. soil, China has long been waging war against the Homeland via cyberattacks. At least that's what the media claim.

Terry D. Wittenmyer made a couple bombshell comments on this issue in his book *Fearing China*:

> **"If cyberattacks are the greatest threats to our security, then we've made great progress since the days school children practiced taking cover under their desks as protection against Soviet nuclear weapons."**

Wittenmyer also wrote, "We need to stop using insecure technologies."

LOL! Is he talking about Mickeysoft?

After I became a political activist in the mid-1990s, people began hacking my websites. When I sought help, someone suggested that I scrap my Microsoft servers, upgrading to Linux servers. It fixed the problem. That still left me with countless bugs and viruses in my PC. I fixed that problem by upgrading to a Mac. Fuck Microsoft.

And how many notifications have I received from various agencies and corporations notifying me that their security was breached and my personal data had been compromised? I've lost count, but I doubt that China was behind any of those incidents.

In fact, the conspiracy theorist in me strongly suggests that some of these incidents are false flag attacks. In other words, corporations may deliberately compromise their own data, allowing them to exploit that data for themselves.

But back to China.

Cyber warfare is a complex thing. Hackers have many strategies for masking their identity or spoofing other people's. It can thus be notoriously difficult to trace a cyberattack to a particular country, let alone individual. If U.S. officials were clueless about Iraq's mythical weapons of mass destruction, how can we trust them when they rant about cyberattacks emanating from China or Russia?

On top of that, U.S. politicians, media whores and corporate personnel are filthy liars. Every time they cry "Chinese cyberattack!" my first thought is "Yeah, right."

Consider the Russians who supposedly hacked the 2016 pResidential election. What an absurd story! U.S. presidential elections are conspiratorial clusterfucks to begin with. They're hacked from the inside.

Which isn't to say the Chinese have never engaged in cyber warfare. Given the fact that the U.S. is a leader in cyber warfare, combined with the military ships and aircraft that are continuously probing mainland China for its most intimate secrets, why shouldn't they? I would love to see the Chinese steal all of Microsoft's secrets and toast Google.

In summary, maybe we should clean up our act before we criticize China. And if the U.S. starts WWIII, let's hope China retaliates with a massive cyberattack that fries Google and Facebook instead of a nuclear attack. And if it does choose the latter option, let's hope it nukes Google, Facebook and Seattle's Microsoft campus.

In the meantime, if you're using a PC running Windows, don't complain about foreign hackers. Upgrade to a Mac and join me in waiting for the day when we can buy even more secure computers loaded with operating systems made in China.

<u>HARMONY</u>

HarmonyOS is a potent symbol of China's technological prowess.

HarmonyOS is a new computer operating system developed by the Chinese telecom giant Huawei. What makes it cool is the mere fact that it exists.

For far too long, the global IT industry has been dominated by Microsoft and Apple, with a relative handful of geeks using Linux. Android is a variety of Linux developed for use on mobile devices by a consortium of developers commercially sponsored by Google.

And that has long been the end of it. Consumers were free to buy computers running Microsoft Windows—a commercial term for crapware—or they could pay an arm and a leg for a Mac. The third option was to dive into the world of Linux, which was unfortunately largely hamstrung by the Microsoft quasi-monopoly.

After pResident Donald Trump declared war on Huawei, the company bravely fought back as best it could. It speeded up the development of HarmonyOS, which now has over 200 million users, mostly in China.

In 2022, HarmonyOS will be released on devices sold outside China. How long do you think it will be before it surpasses Google's Android in popularity?

For billions of people around the world, HarmonyOS represents choice. It will almost certainly be less expensive than Windows, and consumers won't need expensive Macs to run it.

HarmonyOS will operate a wide variety of devices, including laptops, smart phones and even cars.

Another bonus: Security.

If you trust Microsoft, Apple or Google, you're a fool. The U. S. corporate sector is mired in corruption and conspiracy. Surveillance is a huge part of Microsoft's and Google's game plan. That's probably largely true of Apple as well.

China claims that it is interested in commerce, not surveillance. If actions speak louder than words, the Chinese appear to be speaking the truth.

Even if HarmonyOS did become a vehicle for surveillance, how serious could it be compared to Microsoft and Google? I'd much rather be spied on by China than by my own government and operating system vendor.

In the meantime, there is another Chinese operating system worth keeping tabs on—Euler.

The name sounds a little lame to me, but my editor informed me that it commemorates a genius mathematician. More important, this OS may soon be competing with Microsoft Windows and Apple's Mac OS, both of which have gone unchallenged for far too long.

Merely driving Microsoft and Apple out of China will be an exciting accomplishment. If Asian laptops running Euler then begin appearing in stores in Europe, Latin America and Africa, watch out.

BEYOND HARMONY

OF COURSE, CHINA'S HIGH-TECH juggernaut goes far beyond HarmonyOS, and there is some cause for concern.

Fortunately, military applications aren't too worrisome—for me, at least.

Yes, the global arms race is a very sad and frightening thing. But I feel much better knowing the U.S. is no longer king of the hill.

Ironically, a more powerful Chinese military could actually make the world a much safer place. I would certainly predict fewer wars as the U.S. is forced to learn its place.

But it would be foolish to blindly assume that all Chinese technology is good technology. What about artificial intelligence (AI)?

In fact, AI is a scary thing no matter who controls it.

Scientists and philosophers are still trying to understand AI. Can it be good? Can it be controlled? What if just one bad actor decides to harness AI for evil?

I will say that I would greatly prefer to see AI mastered by China than the U.S., whose track record is simply too dismal.

SILICON CHIPS WAR

ONE OF MODERN HISTORY'S strangest sagas has to be the great silicon chip war. Where do I even begin?

As you may know, silicon chips (aka integrated circuits or semiconductors), as you may know, can be likened to artificial brain cells that power various electronic devices, particularly computers and cell phones. They are measured in nanometers, and the smaller ones are more valuable, simply because more of them can be squeezed into a device.

A nanometer, by the way, equals one *billionth* of a meter. In 2021, the smallest silicon chips measured just 2 nanometers. If you're wondering how it's possible to construct, let alone modify, something that small, join the crowd.

Not surprisingly, silicon chips are amazingly complex and difficult to work with. Their manufacture requires multiple processes involving numerous companies and specially designed machines.

The U.S. has long been a leader in silicon chip production. However, it by no means enjoys a monopoly. Taiwan and South Korea are also heavyweights.

Intel is an American multinational company headquartered in Santa Clara, California. It is the world's largest semiconductor chip manufacturer by revenue.

Samsung is South Korea's largest business conglomerate.

Taiwan Semiconductor Manufacturing Company, Limited (TSMC) is a multinational semiconductor contract manufacturing and design company. It is the world's largest dedicated independent semiconductor foundry and the world's most valuable semiconductor company. As you can guess from the name, it is located on Taiwan, the island claimed by China.

However, none of these companies could survive without a great deal of help from multiple countries.

A Dutch firm named ASML is the only company in the world capable of making the highly complex lithography machines that are needed to manufacture the most advanced chips. It sells these machines to a handful of chip giants including TSMC, Samsung and Intel for approximately $140 million each.

ASML has a market value of around $350 billion and growing.

China is the high-tech juggernaut that appears to be missing in action. It was not an early pioneer in semiconductor chip manufacture—a fantastically complex and competitive industry that can take years to master—and more or less got caught with its pants down when pResident Donald Trump declared war on Huawei.

The U.S. government issued an edict that certain Chinese companies aren't allowed to use any silicon chip components or processes that incorporate U.S. technology. That means Huawei can no longer buy chips from Taiwan. The U.S. is also making sure the Dutch firm ASML doesn't sell its most specialized lithography machines to China.

China fought back bravely, making massive investments in silicon chip research. However, the results appear to be mixed.

On the positive side, China is reportedly manufacturing more low-end chips. The bad news is that China so far hasn't been able to manufacture the smaller cutting-edge chips. At the same time, the industry continues to advance in other countries, potentially leaving China even further behind.

In the meantime, there is a global chip shortage that is causing all kinds of problems. It was apparently caused by the U.S. when it took its wrecking ball to China. The U.S. government's knee-jerk war has reportedly had a devastating impact on the entire industry, hurting silicon chip giants like TSMC and diverse companies in the U.S. itself.

SILICON CHIPS ARE SAID TO BE MORE VALUABLE THAN FOSSIL FUELS. THEY ARE THE KEY TO BOTH COMMERCIAL AND MILITARY DOMINANCE.

And so we're left with this grim visage of China, a high-tech juggernaut, left stranded like a beached whale without the high-end silicon chips it needs to compete. And there doesn't appear to be a light at the end of the tunnel yet.

So where will this strange saga end? Surely, China should be able to solve its problem in ten years; but ten years is a hellluva long time in the world of technology. Will China be able to manufacture cutting-edge silicon chips by 2025? If so, how? Will they just figure it out one step at a time? Or will they discover some radical new technology, perhaps improving the process to boot?

Another possibility is that some countries or commercial entities may finally give the U.S. the middle finger and jump ship for China. Alternatively, perhaps China will figure out a way to strike back at the U.S., forcing it to capitulate.

The most intriguing possibility of all might be the reunification of Taiwan with China. If China were able to take control of TSMC, it would be in much better shape.

But would that be the final solution, or would the U.S. still be able to deprive China of critical technology? If the answer is yes, then could China leverage TSMC against the U.S. in return?

THE U.S. IS PRESSURING FOREIGN SEMICONDUCTOR COMPANIES TO SET UP FACILITIES ON ITS HOME TURF EVEN AS IT PRESSURES THEM TO HAND OVER DATA ON THEIR CUSTOMERS. SUCH DIRTY, SELF-SERVING TACTICS MIGHT HELP MOTIVATE FORMER ALLIES TO ABANDON SHIP AND WORK WITH CHINA.

If we really want to go out on a limb, we might imagine a scenario where China invades Taiwan and appears to be on the verge of winning. Desperate to keep China's high-tech industry on its knees, the U.S. blows up TSMC.

Ironically, such an act would probably have a devastating impact on the global high-tech industry. The U.S. would likely be shooting itself in the foot.

The final irony would be a simple end-run around the competition.

In fact, there are reports that China is focusing on carbon-based chips, which are said to be three times faster and four times more energy-efficient than silicon chips. Imagine if China became the global leader in carbon-based chips, which would quickly make silicon chips obsolete.

Do you think China could accomplish that by 2030?

MEDIA BLACKOUT?

If you take an interest in the global computer chip saga, as I have, you may find the news puzzling.

Of course, Western media whores are prone to cheering whenever there's bad news coming out of China, like a slump in Huawei's smart phone sales. But they offer very little good news.

In fact, it seems strangely difficult to find any solid information about the progress China is making.

Eventually, I discovered that one of the best sources of information is YouTube. I hate to promote YouTube, which is owned by Google, but there are some people and organizations there who are publishing interesting news about China's drive for silicon chip independence, along with carbon-based chips.

The quality of the videos is all over the map, and it can be very hard to verify them. Merely understanding them can be difficult.

But it appears that there is at least some truth percolating through these videos. For example, some videos talk about a new technique China is pursuing called photonic lithography. One day I discovered an article in the mainstream media quoting an ASML executive who admitted that the new field of photonics has potential.

There are also reports that ASML isn't happy with Team USA's tech war. The company is effectively losing hundreds of millions of dollars on lost sales to China, money desperately needed for research and development.

At the same time, there are fears that China will create new technology that will compete with ASML or make it less relevant, thanks largely to the U.S.

In the meantime, only time will tell how accurate those YouTube videos are. If some of the things they discuss actually come to pass, the mainstream media will be forced to discuss them at some point.

Stay tuned.

In summary, I find China's technology juggernaut preferable to the U.S. tech industry, though it is not without some concerns.

In the meantime, I can't wait for the day when I can own both a laptop and smart phone running HarmonyOS, with my laptop, in particular, loaded with my favorite software, like Adobe Creative Suite.

Then again, Asian vendors may soon take on Adobe, too. Isn't fair competition and free choice a wonderful thing?

Although the U.S. trade war with China has been brewing for some time, the defining moment for many was delivered by pResident Donald Trump when he all but declared war on Chinese telecom giant Huawei. Indeed, Trump unleashed a flurry of attacks against Huawei, seemingly throwing everything but the kitchen sink at it.

Corporate entities that use U.S. technology were forbidden from working with Huawei, which was deemed a global security risk. For good measure, Meng Wanzhou—daughter of Huawei CEO Ren Zhengfei—was arrested on behalf of U.S. officials at Vancouver

International Airport on December 1, 2018. A year later (January 28, 2019), the U.S. Department of Justice announced financial fraud charges against Meng, accusing her of employing a subsidiary to facilitate business activities in Iran in violation of U.S sanctions.

MENG WANZHOU (CC—SEE CREDITS)

Wanzhou remained under house arrest until after September 24, 2021, when the Department of Justice announced it had reached a deal with Meng to resolve the case through a deferred prosecution agreement.

As part of the deal, Meng agreed to a statement of facts, including a statement that she had made untrue statements to HSBC to enable transactions in the U.S., at least some of which supported Huawei's work in Iran, which violated U.S. law, but she did not have to pay a fine nor plead guilty to her key charges. The Department of Justice said it would move to dismiss all charges against Meng when the deferral period ends on 21 December 2022, on the condition that Meng does not commit any other crimes before then.

Meng finally left Canada for China on September 24, 2021.

Wow, that script reads like some sort of Frankenstein novel!

For starters, who gave the U.S. the authority to levy sanctions against countries against which it has an axe to grind? And what gives the U.S. the authority to force other countries to abide by its sleazy sanctions?

Suppose Argentina imposed sanctions on Israel over its endless war crimes. Would the U.S. be allowed to do business with Israel and give it financial and military aid?

Second, who the hell determined that Huawei is a security risk?

The U.S. sanctions have proved a boon to Nokia and Ericsson, the only European manufacturers of 5G equipment. Nevertheless, the global leader remains China's Huawei, even though U.S. sanctions have hurt it outside China.

So, to put it in perspective, suppose you have two options: install Huawei 5G or opt for Nokia or Ericsson instead. Which would be the most ethical or practical choice?

THE UNITED STATES AND ITS PARTNERS IN CRIME, THE UNITED KINGDOM AND AUSTRALIA, HAVE TAKEN ACTIONS TO RESTRICT OR ELIMINATE THE USE OF CHINESE EQUIPMENT IN THEIR RESPECTIVE 5G NETWORKS. YET THEY TURN A BLIND EYE TO MICROSOFT, APPLE, GOOGLE, AND THE SOCIAL NETWORKS THAT HAVE REPLACED FREE SPEECH WITH A "CANCEL CULTURE."

The U.S. and its partners in crime are clearly playing dirty pool. They make wild, unsubstantiated accusations alleging that Huawei is a security risk joined at the hip with China's authoritarian government.

Just suppose the U.S. Chamber of Commerce was, for once, telling the truth. What would be the ramifications?

For example, imagine making a phone call with your Huawei

smartphone over a Huawei 5G installation. You talk to a friend about your job, the weather, and the upcoming World Cup soccer games.

However, the evil Chinese Communist Party is eavesdropping on your conversation. The authoritarian thugs now know all about the weather in your neighborhood. They have intelligence that you may not be happy with your job, and they know who your favorite World Cup team is. What next?

Are assassins working for the Chinese Communist Party going to crash into your home in Latin America or—assuming Huawei 5G was allowed in the U.S.—Gothic Seattle and slit your throat? Are they going to persuade you to vote for their preferred political candidate? Are they going to motivate you to support an up and coming Chinese invasion of Mexico or Switzerland?

Even if Huawei 5G was less than trustworthy, China simply doesn't have that kind of track record. Instead, it is the U.S. government and corporate sector that spy on people around the world. Why do you think Google has that office in the Pentagon? To what extent has Bill Gates worked with the CIA? Facebook, Twitter and other U.S. social networks are key dispensers of propaganda and surveillance. They are the architects of corporate corruption, terrorism and war, not China.

While the U.S. has largely succeeded in purging Huawei from Europe, it has been much less successful in Latin America.

While the U.S. clumsily sought to extricate itself from its sleazy occupation of Afghanistan, China took the initiative in delivering COVID-19 vaccines in Latin America. In lieu of the United States' phony democracy, China has performed a useful, humanitarian service that will still further shore up Huawei's 5G initiative, helping it win a race fundamental to the course of the century.

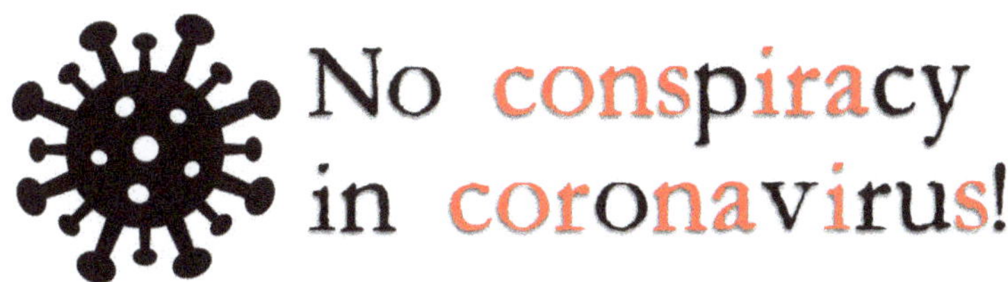

Few issues underscore the differences between the U.S. and China better than the coronavirus pandemic.

While the United States' handling of the pandemic has earned it global scorn, China has earned rave reviews for dealing with it quickly, professionally and ethically. China has also helped other countries cope with the coronavirus, while the U.S. has exploited it as a weapon against states it doesn't like, including Venezuela, Iran and Syria.

Then there's the blame game.

The U.S. insists that the coronavirus originated in China, probably in a lab in Wuhan. Are U.S. officials insinuating the Chinese intentionally created COVID-19 as some kind of bioweapon? If so, doesn't that sound kind of like a C-O-N-S-P-I-R-A-C-Y T-H-E-O-R-Y?

The irony lies in the fact that discussing conspiracy theories in the U.S. is increasingly dangerous. Saying the wrong things about the coronavirus pandemic can get you banned by Google, Facebook or Twitter—or worse. Some people who publicly discuss conspiracy theories may find themselves being fired. Some may lose their entire careers. The media are also increasingly warning that people who discuss conspiracy theories can be sued, driving the point home with a bizarre series of lawsuits against Alex Jones, who is not an authentic conspiracy analyst.

(If you're an Alex Jones fan, I hope you won't be offended. I simply find it odd that an authentic conspiracy expert would be given so much publicity by the corporate media. In addition, some of Jones' ideas are downright wacko. However, this is a topic I explore in much greater detail in my books about conspiracy.)

Some people claim there's tantalizing evidence that COVID-19 was actually created in a lab in the U.S. Some have even suggested that COVID-19 was created as a bioweapon for use against China. In fact, I know of one particular book that does a pretty good job of exploring some of these theories.

But if I mention this book, will the book you're reading be banned by Amazon and other booksellers?

If you would like to learn more about my research and views on the global coronavirus pandemic, please contact me. I promise I won't report you to Facebook or the CIA. ;)

WAR!

Towards the end of 2021, it looked like China might win the Great Game without firing a shot. The Chinese simply took control of the global marketplace while the U.S. squandered its resources on a bloated military, pampered upper class, and pointless wars in the Middle East. The U.S. is now fighting back, but it may be too little too late.

And that worries people who think a desperate U.S. might opt for a military solution. However, China has been hard at work beefing up its military, and it's hard to imagine China's government allowing the U.S. to bully their country into submission.

So does that mean we're going to have a ringside seat for World

War III, or will there be no war at all? Alternatively, will China and the U.S. fight a limited conventional war?

Anyone who tells you they know for a fact that there will or will not be a war is almost as big a fool as those who claim they know who will win. There are simply too many variables, and the playing field changes daily. In the meantime, the media continue pumping out the most idiotic bullshit. One of my favorites is the claim that China has slightly more ships than the U.S., but it's no big deal because the U.S. boasts greater total tonnage and better technology.

What the morons forget to mention is the fact that much of the U.S. Navy is stationed in the Atlantic Ocean.

The U.S. Atlantic fleet is the invisible elephant in the other room.

On November 20, 2021, I checked Wikipedia's "List of current ships of the United States Navy." It lists 250 commissioned ships, including 136 stationed in the Pacific Ocean versus 114 in the Atlantic. That's well over a third of commissioned ships assigned to the Atlantic Ocean.

Of course, if World War III breaks out, our fearless commander-in-chief will likely order some ships from the Atlantic to head for the Pacific, but they have to leave some ships to support their fools' errands in the Middle East, along with ships to intimidate Russia and terrorize various countries bordering the Atlantic.

In summary, it appears that the U.S. Navy will be terrorizing China with approximately two thirds of its fleet, which would give China a whopping advantage in numbers.

But I'm getting ahead of myself. Let's back up and explore the likelihood of a war between China and the U.S. before we tackle the million-dollar question, "Who would win?"

<u>WILL THERE BE WAR?</u>

THIS IS A QUESTION that renews itself on the first day of each year. If war doesn't happen in 2021, there's a chance it might happen in 2022. If peace reigns in 2022, then we can brace for war in 2023, 2025 and on and on.

But the cycle can't continue forever. The day will come when the U.S. is no longer capable of fighting major wars. Someday the U.S. won't even exist. Maybe China will split into three different countries in the 22nd century. There's no guarantee the human species will even survive this century.

So, just to make our question a little more meaningful, let's explore the possibility of war between China and the U.S. by the year 2030. That's nearly a decade away, and the global playing field will probably be very different from today.

YES, THERE WILL BE WAR

If war becomes a reality, then it must follow certain parameters. So let's take a closer look with three more detailed questions:

1. Who will start it?
2. How will it start?
3. When will it start?

1. WHO WILL START IT?

There are logically two primary answers: China or the United States.

But there are other possibilities.

Any U.S. ally with a presence in the region could start a war, notably India. There are European war ships patrolling the South China Sea as well.

However, I don't think it's likely a U.S. ally would deliberately start a war with China, for two simple reasons. First, no U.S. ally has sufficient strength to challenge China militarily by itself. Second, any ally counting on support from the U.S. would be foolish. America's military résumé is looking increasingly tattered, and let's not forget that its losing streak is strongest in Asia (e.g. Vietnam and Afghanistan). Moreover, it was China that stopped the U.S. in its tracks during the Korean War, when China's military was vastly weaker than it is today.

Realistically, that leaves us with two primary antagonists, the U.S. and China. Logically, it doesn't seem likely that China would start a war when it's already winning through its economic and technological prowess. The U.S. is clearly the country that is pushing for war, and it is the country that would most likely start a war, with one notable exception.

There's a very real possibility that China might decide to take Taiwan back by force, which would obviously start a war between China and Taiwan. If the U.S. responded by launching a military attack against China, who would we then blame for starting World War III—the U.S. or China?

2. HOW WILL IT START?

This is even tougher than the first question.

For starters, a war could be started intentionally or accidentally.
ACCIDENTAL WAR?
As the U.S. and its allies continue recruiting ships to police China's coastal waters and nearby seas, the risk of accidents obviously increases.

On October 2, 2021, the *USS Connecticut* was damaged after it reportedly collided with an unknown object in the South China

Sea. Eleven crew members reportedly suffered minor injuries on the $3-billion-dollar nuclear powered submarine.

The *Connecticut* limped to Guam for repairs, and three key personnel were relieved of their duties—Commander Cameron Aljilani (the commanding officer), Lieutenant Commander Patrick Cashin, and Master Chief Sonar Technician Cory Rodgers.

The U.S. Navy's claim that the submarine had struck an underwater mountain had people around the world scratching their heads in disbelief, especially when the Navy refused to reveal the location. There were later claims that the sub may have hit an abandoned oil rig.

Could it have been rammed by a Chinese submarine?

Two U.S. submarines, the *USS Thresher* and *USS Scorpion*, were lost with all hands in 1963 and 1968, respectively. The U.S. Navy lied about the cause of both incidents. In fact, both submarines were rammed by Soviet subs. France, Israel and the Soviet Union have also lost submarines.

In more recent years, several U.S. submarines have struck underwater objects or even become grounded, like beached whales. (See "How did a $3 billion US Navy submarine hit an undersea mountain?," Brad Lendon, CNN, November 4, 2021)

Imagine if a nuclear sub suffered such an accident, and its nuclear reactor was damaged. It could turn into a deep-sea version of Chernobyl or Fukushima, or perhaps it could occur near a coral reef or valuable coastal fishery.

Not long before this book was published, seven U.S. military personnel were injured when an F-35 crashed while landing on the *USS Carl Vinson* in the South China Sea. The aircraft sank to the bottom of the sea, prompting the U.S. to launch a frantic effort to recover it before China could retrieve it.

If the U.S. starts a war, they'll be operating in a far more stressful and crazier environment.

But wayward submarines and aircraft crashes aren't the only problem. The U.S. government has persuaded several allies to dispatch ships, including aircraft carriers, to the Western Pacific in a show of might (or intimidation). In fact, a number of war games have been conducted in the western Pacific.

The U.S. has also been supplying Taiwan with arms. U.S. troops have even been deployed to Taiwan. At the same time, China continues increasing its harassment of Taiwan.

With all those ships, submarines, aircraft and clandestine military personnel playing games, there's plenty that could go wrong. And don't forget the aerial drones, underwater drones, experimental robots, satellites and artificial intelligence that are under continual development. The entire battlefield—which includes land, sea, space, the laboratory and the Internet—is a moving target.

INTENTIONAL WAR?

I already stated my belief that it's unlikely that a U.S. ally would provoke a war with China, though there are notable tensions between China and India.

I also think it's extremely unlikely that China would start a war—unless it attempted to force Taiwan back into the fold.

A war between China and Taiwan could start in a number of ways. China might target Taiwan with missiles or bombs, or it might dispatch an invasion fleet. It could also attempt to blockade Taiwan.

In any event, the U.S. would then have the option of deciding if it wants to defend Taiwan.

Of course, no one has more experience at starting wars than the U.S., and there are countless ways the U.S. could start a war with China.

The U.S. could attack a Chinese asset, or it could trick Chinese observers into thinking they're under attack.

The U.S. could also arrange a false flag attack, similar to the sinking of the battleship *USS Maine* in Cuba in 1898 or the 9/11 terrorist attacks. American media whores exploited the *Maine* in agitating for the Spanish American War, while 9/11 was used to justify a phony international war on terror.

Following tradition, the U.S. could blow up one of its own ships, submarines or airplanes and blame it on China. Or it could falsely accuse China of blowing up a U.S. satellite or launching a major cyberattack.

But there's a pillar of irony that may discourage the U.S. from starting a war with China.

Team USA's biggest nightmare is the reunification of Taiwan with China. The irony is that starting a war with China would give it the excuse it needs to take back Taiwan.

PROVOKING A WAR WITH CHINA MIGHT ONLY ENCOURAGE A CHINESE INVASION OF TAIWAN.

Taiwan, after all, is a U.S. ally. If a war broke out between China and the U.S., one would expect the U.S. to further militarize Taiwan, and the Chinese would be stupid not to not treat Taiwan as a threat.

This logic suggests to me that the U.S. would be very reluctant to openly start a war with China. Theoretically, it would instead muddy the waters, starting a war through some kind of trickery, then blaming the war on China.

3. WHEN WILL IT START?

This question is impossible to answer with any certainty, but we can take a stab at it.

For me, it is all to do with trends and trajectories. China is clearly a rapidly rising power, while the U.S. increasingly looks like a sinking ship.

Indeed, the U.S. has frantically recruited Japan, the Philippines, India, Australia, the United Kingdom and Germany to help it keep China on a leash. The U.S. clearly cannot do the job alone.

This suggests that time is on China's side. China will be significantly stronger in 2022 than it was in 2021, and it will be stronger still in 2023. If China already has more ships than the U.S., how many ships will it have by 2024?

China's economy is expected to match the United States' economy shortly after 2025. Imagine how powerful China will be if it masters the art of manufacturing high-end semiconductors.

Therefore, if the U.S. wants to start a war with China, it had better act quick. Following this line of reasoning, the likelihood of the U.S. starting a war with China should diminish each year, until the U.S. abandons all hope of ever besting China in a war.

On the other hand, a growing mismatch in power may encourage China to pounce on Taiwan, an act that might force America's hand.

In other words, in 2025, the U.S. will presumably be less inclined to start a war, but China might be more inclined to attack Taiwan.

I'll go out on a limb and predict that China will attempt to annex Taiwan by 2030 and quite probably by 2025. If the U.S. doesn't interfere, Taiwan will almost certainly become part of the empire once again. The return of Taiwan would significantly increase China's power, making an attack by the U.S. even more unlikely.

If, on the other hand, the U.S. decides to defend Taiwan, then who knows what will happen? About the only thing we can (almost) guarantee is that it will be a helluva long time before China and the U.S. fight another war. In fact, it could be history's last war, period.

Of course, I could be dead wrong.

Some observers claim China's phenomenal growth is about to slow down. According to some, China may remain powerful for about a decade before it starts sliding downhill. This state of affairs would supposedly give China an incentive to attack Taiwan while it has sufficient power.

Then again, there's a carnival of fools predicting the end of China every day. I'll believe it when I see it.

However, even if China does go into a sudden decline, that won't necessarily change the big picture.

In fact, many people believe the U.S. has been in decline for some time. The U.S. is increasingly hated. Its inability to defeat countries like Vietnam and Afghanistan make it look weak and foolish, and it now has to contend with China on a growing number of fronts.

Claims that China's population is on the verge of collapsing are echoed in the U.S., which reported the lowest per capita birth rate in its entire history in 2021. Are Americans going to go the way of the dodo?

In summary, we are living in strange times, and we can't really predict the future, for either China or the U.S.

However, China has been steadily growing in power for more than half a century, while the U.S. appears to be moving in the opposite direction. Draw your own conclusions.

NO WAR?

There are many observers and armchair military buffs who insist there will be no war between the U.S. and China. Below are three facts supporting such a conclusion.

1. China is simply too powerful for the U.S. to attack with any certainty of victory.

2. The U.S. economy is too dependent on China; an attack on China could thus damage the U.S. at the same time.

3. A war between the two countries could easily provoke a nuclear exchange, potentially unleashing far more destruction than World War II.

The implications are enormous.

The U.S. and its allies have traditionally cut rival powers down to size. Both world wars were essentially power struggles pitting the U.S. and Western Europe (along with Russia and the Soviet Union) against Germany and its allies. After WWII, the U.S. and its allies were preoccupied with clipping the Soviet Union's wings.

Even less powerful countries that refuse to do the Empire's bidding are targeted for sanctions or military invasion. Examples include Cuba, Venezuela, Argentina, Iran and Libya.

A few countries that refuse to kowtow to the U.S. Chamber of Commerce have so far survived (e.g. Cuba and Venezuela), and a few have even defeated the U.S. military (e.g. Vietnam and Afghanistan). But Vietnam and Afghanistan fought the U.S. with guerrilla warfare, and all four countries listed above paid dearly for their independence.

No country has defied the U.S. more boldly or successfully than China, which has, in some observers' opinion, effectively turned the U.S. into its colony.

In plain English, China may have succeeded where Adolf Hitler and Joseph Stalin failed. Surely, such a feat deserves respect. But that's just the tip of the iceberg, because China may make it more difficult for the U.S. to exploit and attack weaker countries as well.

There may be no better example than Afghanistan. As mentioned, many observers have opined that the U.S. was effectively forced to retreat from Afghanistan in order to marshal its forces against China.

I'm hoping that China will supply Iran and Syria with weapons that will help them stand up to Israel, the U.S. and their allies. When greater numbers of U.S. troops begin coming home in bodybags, victims of weapons made in China, maybe the U.S. government will think twice about invading other countries. And maybe ordinary citizens will think twice about enlisting in the U.S. military.

In the meantime, China may have already become too powerful for the U.S. to mess with. And since the Chinese appear to have no interest in starting a war, that could be a recipe for peace.

WHO WILL WIN?

ALTHOUGH I'LL PROUDLY CHEER for China, I wouldn't bet money on either side. There are simply too many variables, many of them highly complex.

Let's start by taking a look at each side's primary strengths and weaknesses.

U.S. ADVANTAGES

The U.S. has the most powerful military in the world. It also has a wealth of experience, having fought wars all over the world, including both world wars. In comparison, China has amazingly little experience fighting wars.

America's Asian wars include World War II, Korea, Vietnam and Afghanistan.

The U.S. also boasts the world's biggest economy, and its political and cultural clout are similarly overwhelming. Not surprisingly, it has many allies, including Canada, most of Europe, Israel, Australia, India and Japan.

China borders just one ocean, and it is largely boxed in by islands controlled by the U.S. or its allies, including Japan, Taiwan and the

Philippines. The U.S. also has military assets in the middle of the Pacific Ocean (e.g. Guam).

A war between the two countries would probably see a U.S. fleet massed near China, where it would be free to inflict damage on the country. In contrast, China would almost certainly not be able to threaten the U.S. Pacific Coast with a similar fleet, and the East Coast would be even further removed from danger.

The U.S. could also seek to attack China via some of the countries that border it, particularly in the south and west.

THE U.S. IS THE ULTIMATE WAR WHORE.

The U.S. also has a reputation for playing dirty. It is the only country that has actually used atomic bombs in time of war. The WWII fire bombings of Dresden, Germany and Tokyo, Japan were equally horrendous war crimes.

During the Korean War, the U.S. carpet-bombed North Korea. It was also accused of using biological weapons against North Korean and Chinese troops.

After launching its phony war on terror in the wake of 9/11, the U.S. openly embraced torture. pResident Obama further popularized unmanned drones as instruments of assassination, even when many, if not all, of the victims were innocent civilians.

If war broke out between the U.S. and China, China would be smart to be prepared for dirty tricks including efforts to wipe out China's food supply, condemning millions of people to starvation.

CHINESE ADVANTAGES

China is commonly said to have the third most powerful military in the world, after Russia. However, the engine that drives military growth is a country'e economy, and China's economy leaves Russia's in the dust.

Some say China's military won't be on a par with the United States until 2050, a claim that should be taken with a huge grain of salt. It remains to be seen if the U.S. will even be standing on its feet by 2030.

Keep in mind, also, that the U.S. got its ass kicked by Vietnam and Afghanistan, neither of which is nearly as powerful as China. China also fought the U.S. to a standstill in Korea in the 1950s, when China was just a Third World power.

China may be behind the U.S. when it comes to allies, but take a closer look. North Korea would probably side with China. China might also neutralize Taiwan rapidly.

India has a powerful military, but it has a corrupt government and economic sector, similar to the U.S. Moreover, India is bordered on the west by Pakistan, a nuclear power that has long been a bitter enemy. If India sides with the U.S. against China but Pakistan weighs in on China's side, watch out.

However, the real wild card may be Russia. Persecution by the U.S. has driven Russia and China closer together, and Russia would make one powerful ally. But can it be trusted? Russian strongman Vladimir Putin is awfully cozy with Israel, which is a staunch U.S. ally.

In the meantime, it isn't clear how committed America's allies will be. Many Europeans are sitting on the fence over the U.S.-China trade war, and many would prefer to do business with China. At the same time, generations of lies, betrayal, spying, bloody wars and the byproducts of wars (e.g. refugees) have given the U.S. a black eye. Anyone stupid enough to support the U.S. deserves to get bombed back to the 19th century.

Yes, China is boxed in, but the Chinese would be fighting for their homeland. Western propagandists can spin all the lies they want, but it will be hard to cast China as the aggressor when it's fighting in its backyard.

The U.S. will have to move its war machine across the Pacific, while China's will be set up and ready to rock and roll.

While the over-extended U.S. has to plan for incidents around the world, China is focused primarily on defending itself against the U.S.

AMERICA'S VAST ARMADA OF TANKS WOULD PROBABLY BE USELESS IN WHAT WOULD LIKELY BE A MARITIME AND AIR WAR.

China is now said to have the world's largest navy. In 2021, the U.S. Office of Naval Intelligence said China had about 360 ships compared to 297 for the U.S.

By 2025, China is expected to have as many as 400 vessels compared to 355 U.S. vessels. Some sources predict China will have 460 ships by 2030.

Right-wing armchair patriots laugh off this imbalance, claiming that American ships are bigger and more technologically advanced. At the same time, U.S. allies will also beef up an invasion fleet.

But as we've seen, not all of America's ships are deployed in the Pacific. If war broke out today, and one third of the U.S. fleet remained in the Atlantic Ocean, that would leave 200 U.S. ships to take on 350 Chinese ships or more.

The global arms race is proceeding at breakneck speed. With the U.S., Russia, China and other countries continuously leapfrogging each other and making new technological breakthroughs, it's very difficult to predict which country might be ahead in a particular arena (e.g. stealth bombers or underwater drones) next year or five years down the road.

However, China's militarization efforts should not be taken lightly. China has made enormous progress on many different fronts. At the same time, the U.S. government can't possibly know all there is to know about China's military research and development or strategies. Bear in mind that the same technological prowess that has made China such a potent economic competitor buoys its militarization efforts.

China would also presumably have an advantage in troop morale.

American troops are brave when they're carrying state of the art weapons and communications gear, wearing body armor, and backed up by helicopter gunships and cruise missiles. However, the U.S. no longer has a commanding lead in military technology. Going up against Chinese troops who are themselves backed up by helicopter gunships, jet fighters, missiles, and drones will be a daunting mission.

Only a fool would expect to defeat China without losing a certain percentage of ships. What would happen to U.S. troop morale if one of those ships were to be an aircraft carrier?

MANY PEOPLE CLAIM THERE WILL NEVER BE A WAR WITH CHINA. THAT SENTIMENT IS ITSELF A TESTAMENT TO CHINA'S POWER.

At the same time, U.S. troops would know they're fighting in another war that doesn't enjoy broad support at home, let alone world-wide. They'll also know that Operation China won't be a cakewalk.

Chinese troops, on the other hand, will be fighting for their homeland, not some vague ideological principle or corporate think tank. While U.S. troops could retreat back across the Pacific, Chinese troops will effectively have nowhere to run.

I predict Chinese morale will be significantly higher.

PEOPLE POWER

Wars aren't won by soldiers alone. For example, it is widely claimed that the Cold War was won by America's economy, which the Soviet Union couldn't compete with.

Of course, guerrilla wars would wither and die without popular support, from Cuba to Palestine.

So, if we pitted America's more than 300 million civilians against China's population of nearly one-and-a-half billion, who would win?

While America is increasingly seen as a nation of trailer park trash and homeless people, China generally has its act together.

Chinese citizens are generally well educated. They have free health care. China doesn't have an army of homeless people dragging it down.

China's infrastructure is also better developed than America's. That would make it much easier for China's government to quickly transport troops and war supplies across vast distances.

The Chinese are arguably a lot tougher than Americans as well. While the U.S. was never really invaded during WWII outside of Pearl Harbor and Alaska's Aleutian Islands, China was invaded by Japanese troops who treated the Chinese mercilessly.

While the U.S. was celebrating the end of WWII, millions of Chinese were starving. The Chinese endured decades of poverty before they created their world-class economy.

In comparison, most Americans are pampered sissies. If China merely fried the Internet, millions of Americans might be ready to throw in the towel within a couple weeks. How long could the average U.S. citizen survive without Google, YouTube or Facebook, which are banned in China?

WILD CARDS

Imagine hundreds of ships and submarines, hundreds of aircraft, thousands of missiles and torpedoes, and thousands of drones—both aerial and aquatic—maneuvering and streaking through the sky and sea. A war between the U.S. and China could be as exciting as it would be unpredictable!

But there are further variables that would make such a war even more unpredictable.

The U.S. fleet would be in a position to inflict damage on mainland China, but it would be much harder for Chinese forces to attack the U.S. mainland.

Difficult, but not impossible. China has submarines and long-range stealth bombers and missiles that can strike the U.S. What impact would a single strike on the U.S. have?

During World War II, Japanese forces bombed Pearl Harbor, Hawaii and invaded Alaska's Aleutian Islands. However, the 48 contiguous states have been virtually untouched by war since the War of 1812. (The obvious exception is the Civil War, then the U.S. was at war with itself.)

If Chinese war strategists wanted to give Americans a taste of war, they would have plenty of targets, including an aging infrastructure. pResident Joe Biden's one-trillion-dollar infrastructure bill will help shore up the country's foundation, but it's really just a drop in the bucket. Renovated or not, there are plenty of major dams and bridges that could be easily destroyed.

A friend who works as a commercial diver once told me Homeland Security asked him for advice on how to prevent terrorists from blowing up dams on the Ohio River. He laughed and said, "good luck," as he told me how one individual could blow up every dam on the Ohio River with some very inexpensive equipment.

A significant attack on U.S. soil would have a profound impact. It could incite cries for nuclear payback, or it could motivate frightened citizens to call off their dogs of war.

A Chinese attack on America wouldn't necessarily have to be military in nature. What would an all-out cyberattack look like? How long could Americans survive without Google, Facebook and their local weather channel? How many businesses could survive without an online presence?

Could a Chinese submarine sneak into the Atlantic Ocean and launch an attack on Washington, D.C.?

In 2021, the media reported rumors that China was looking for a military base in West Africa. Bear in mind, the Atlantic Ocean is much smaller than the Pacific, and Africa's west coast isn't blocked by island chains.

Imagine if China was able to station ships, submarines, aircraft and missiles within striking distance of the U.S. capital!

Another intriguing thought: what if some country in Latin America, the Middle East or even Europe decides to rebel against the New World Order while the U.S. is tied up with a campaign against China?

Could Chinese strategists consider attempting to start a war in another corner of the globe, just to overwhelm the Pentagon?

Imagine if a war between the U.S. and China was interrupted by another war between Iran and Israel. Imagine if various Arab countries began allying with Iran.

A major war in the Middle East could be as explosive as a war between the U.S. and China. Could the U.S. handle both simultaneously?

USA VS USA?

There's one particular scenario that millions of people around the world might find quite humorous.

Everyone knows that an all-out war between the U.S. and China would torpedo both countries' economies. However, many observers predict that China will get hit even harder than the U.S. But take a closer look.

China is far more squared away than the U.S. China's people are more disciplined and united, its infrastructure more robust. Moreover, the Chinese have experienced suffering that Americans can't even imagine, including war and mass starvation.

In contrast, the U.S. is a quagmire. Millions of Americans probably never recovered from pResident George W. Bush, who gave us 9/11 and a second Great Depression.

More recently, U.S. citizens were hammered by the coronavirus pandemic, which saw the rich get richer while everyone else suffered. Americans are also suffering from the global supply chain problems that were created by their own government.

When this book was published, the U.S. was said to be in a recession, with Americans worried about inflation and gasoline that cost over $5 a gallon.

In plain English, we're screwed, even without a war. So, imagine what would happen if the U.S. and China took off the gloves and declared war against each other.

In the wake of George W. Bush and the coronavirus pandemic, we get yet another round of economic mayhem, with countless businesses forced to close and millions of Americans laid off. The unemployment rate could double or triple, and the ranks of the homeless would also increase.

At the same time, the global supply chain would likely melt down, and Americans would experience shortages of all kinds of goods. It would probably be far worse than anything Americans have experienced since the Great Depression. In fact, it could be worse than the Great Depression itself.

With mobs of unemployed and homeless people roaming the streets, America would be ripe for revolution or anarchy. Since contemporary Americans really don't have the brains or backbone for revolution, I would predict the latter.

If you think Americans have enough discipline to stand up to such a punishing economic situation ... well, you could be right. However, do you remember the endless George Floyd riots? Do you think they could happen again? And what about climate change? Imagine if Seattle experienced temperatures of 110 degrees, two or three days in a row.

Keep in mind, also, that millions of people around the world are also going to suffer if the U.S. and China go to war, and who do you think they're going to blame for their suffering? The Chinese haven't been stirring things up; it's the other way around.

In plain English, I think the Chinese have the patience, discipline, and order to survive a punishing war, while the U.S. could quickly and easily disintegrate.

WAR WITHOUT A WINNER?

Of course, we have to consider the possibility that World War III will have no victors. In fact, that's probably the most logical scenario if it turned into a nuclear shootout.

However, even a conventional war could turn both the U.S. and China into wastelands.

World War I lasted from 1914 to 1918, World War II from 1939 to

1945. The two wars combined spanned just three decades, with two decades separating the end of WWI from the beginning of WWII.

Now think of the technological advances that occurred during those three decades.

WWI saw the first use of armored tanks and airplanes, in the form of two-winged biplanes. (Actually, airplanes had also seen limited use during the Italo-Turkish War in 1911.)

Tanks and aircraft were far more advanced during WWII. Aircraft carriers were first used in combat during WWII. During WWII, the Germans were the first to use missiles as well.

The damage resulting from the two atomic bombs the U.S. dropped on Japan at the end of the war was ironically a relative slap in the face. The fire-bombing of Tokyo actually killed more people. No atomic bombs were dropped on Europe, which nevertheless experienced massive devastation, especially in Germany, Poland and the Soviet Union.

Remember, a mere two decades separated the two world wars. That's less than half the three quarters of a century that has elapsed since the end of WWII. And that's just the beginning ...

World War II was followed by the computer age, which increased the very speed of technological advances. We're now living in the age of hypersonic missiles, drones and artificial intelligence. Today, several countries have nuclear weapons, and any one of them could probably destroy civilization alone.

Of course, another possibility is that a war between the U.S. and China could end in a quick draw or ceasefire.

In the end, we really won't know how a war between the U.S. and China will play out until it actually happens. If it does happen, I'll be cheering for China.

REMOTE WAR?

ALAS, EVERYTHING I'VE WRITTEN about war is a product of tunnel vision.

After all, it's hard to imagine China starting a war short of an invasion of Taiwan. And the U.S. and its allies aren't agitating for war in the South China Sea. (Or are they?) Moreover, the idea of China starting a war far from home is almost unthinkable.

Bur what about the U.S.?

Obviously, it would be hard to attack Chinese military assets around the world when there are so few assets to attack. But what about civilian targets? If China's life blood is global trade, then a simple reduction in imports and exports could deal China a crippling blow.

The U.S. and its allies—notably Israel—could kill two birds with one stone by attacking Iran, which has enormous control over the Persian Gulf.

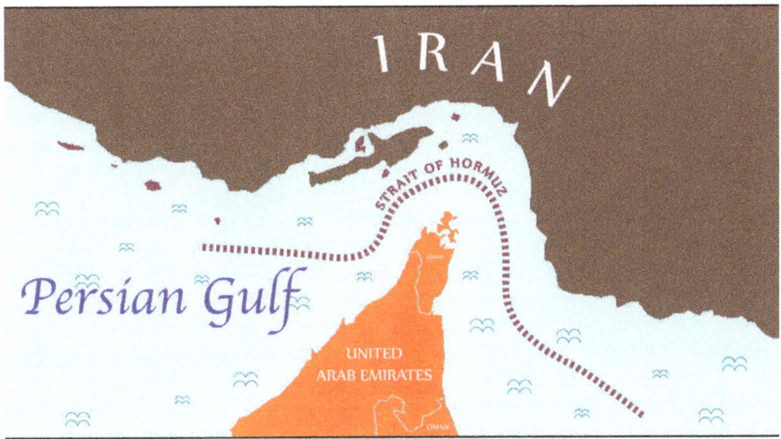

The Persian Gulf is of immense importance to the global economy because of the immense volume of fossil fuels that transit its waters.

The traffic is most vulnerable along the narrow Strait of Hormuz, which connects the Persian Gulf to the Gulf of Oman.

In the event of war, Iran could theoretically block the Strait of Hormuz, dealing its enemies a crippling blow. Unfortunately, blocking oil tankers would cripple Iran's economy at the same time.

However, Iran could build a port on the east side of the Strait of Hormuz, which would allow it to continue shipping oil while blocking oil tankers representing other countries.

Bear in mind that the U.S. has already sanctioned Iran, and that this includes targeting its oil tankers. Israel has been brazenly launching attacks against Iran, even assassinating Iranian officials and scientists inside Iran. At the same time, Iran and China have reportedly forged an alliance, raising the stakes even higher.

At any rate, if Team USA took control of the Persian Gulf and the Strait of Hormuz, they could cripple Iran and China at the same time.

Another notable choke point is the Strait of Malacca, which lies between Malaysia and Indonesia. This strait is the shortest sea route by which to move goods from the Persian Gulf to Asian markets. It is over one-third shorter than the closest alternative sea-based route.

China's government has expressed interest in building a canal in Thailand, which could replace the Strait of Malacca. The canal would connect the Gulf of Thailand with the Andaman Sea across the Kra Isthmus in southern Thailand. However, even if the Thai government gives such a project a green light, it will be years before it could be completed.

Controlling either the Strait of Hormuz or the Strait of Malacca would give the U.S. enormous control over China's economy. The U.S. could also intercept or even destroy ships carrying goods to or from China. Sinking just one cargo ship could serve as a warning, persuading various countries to stop doing business with China.

The U.S. could also initiate military action in various countries that have signed on with China's Belt and Road Initiative. Or they could orchestrate a terrorist attack or proxy war that does the job. ISIS (aka ISIL) is always ready to do the bidding of its masters (the U.S. and Israel).

The ease with which the U.S. could derail China's economy through hard power exercised far from China itself has to be a major headache for Chinese officials. That's doubtless one of the reasons why China is building aircraft carriers and seeking to establish a string of military bases along its trade route.

Simple logic therefore suggests that, if the U.S. wants to sever Chinese trade routes, it would be best to act before China is fully able to protect its far-flung assets.

As mentioned above, China and Iran have forged an alliance, and Syria has signed on with China's Belt and Road Initiative. These events have alarmed and infuriated Israeli war hawks, who have enormous influence over the U.S. government.

I would therefore expect such a war to happen very soon—at any time. Once China has established a string of military bases and has a few operational carrier groups, the U.S. will be more hesitant to try such a stunt. Particularly intriguing is the possibility that China might build a military base (or bases) in Iran, especially one on the southeast side of the Strait of Hormuz.

ENVIRONMENT

What could be worse than World War III?

How about climate change? The global extinction crisis? Genetically modified food?

Combine all the above and add an ocean filled with plastic and all that crappy air people around the world have to breathe, and you have the state of the global environment. How ironic that the coronavirus pandemic actually gave the environment a much needed break, as millions of people around the world stayed home.

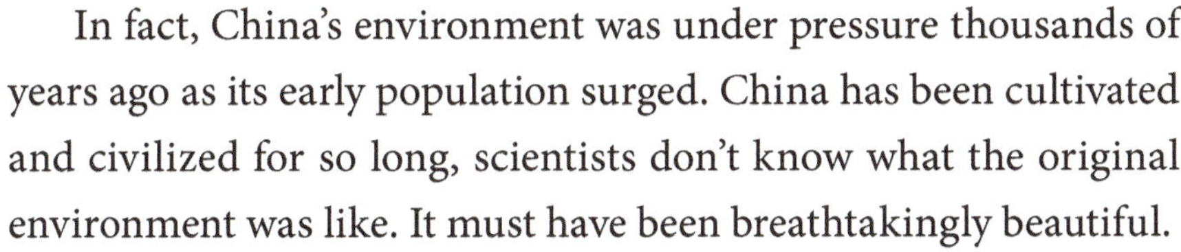

Unfortunately, the environment is one issue where China's track record might not be so rosy.

In fact, China's environment was under pressure thousands of years ago as its early population surged. China has been cultivated and civilized for so long, scientists don't know what the original environment was like. It must have been breathtakingly beautiful.

A list of the 100 cities with the worst air pollution is dominated by China, though there are 13 cities in India that are worse than anything China has to offer. The mere population density of eastern

China is something I couldn't cope with; even the western U.S. is too crowded for me.

Where some Chinese citizens have a hard time breathing, various wild species have a hard time surviving.

The baiji is a species of dolphin native to China's Yangtze River. The last confirmed individual died in 2002, and it is generally believed to be the first dolphin species exterminated by humans.

(CC—SEE CREDITS)

Farther afield, there have been reports of huge Chinese fishing fleets scouring the seas for food, oblivious to the health of the marine ecosystem. The claim that a Chinese "dark" fishing fleet is plundering the ocean sounds pretty ominous ... assuming it's true.

It's hard to find a bright side to this picture. About the best we can do is argue that the U.S. is little, if any, better.

Although early American peoples were probably wiping out native species thousands of years ago, the American Holocaust really gained steam just a few hundred years ago, long after China's environment had already been severely impacted.

Of course, modern Americans have exterminated plenty of

species, including the passenger pigeon. Yankee whalers decimated populations of cetaceans around the world long before China's last baiji took its last breath.

One issue that horrifies me is China's dam-building spree.

China is currently planning on building the world's biggest hydroelectric dam on Tibet's sacred Yarlung Tsangpo. China has already built an enormous dam on the Nile River in Ethiopia. Is nothing sacred?

The Grand Ethiopian Renaissance Dam may be a major political blunder as well; it certainly wasn't well received downstream in Egypt and Sudan.

Ironically, the biggest victim of mega dams could be China itself.

China is the site of the biggest dam-building project ever, the South-North Water Transfer Project, which will take decades to finish. The goal is to channel water from the Yangtze River in southern China to the more arid north through three canal systems.

It sounds logical.

Flooding is a problem in southern China, while northern China has too little water. So why not transfer water from the south to the north?

The biggest irony may be the fact that Chinese officials think dams are good for the environment, if I understand correctly. More precisely, they may be seen as the lesser of evils.

Dams, of course, can be used to produce power. That makes them an alternative to coal. A series of dams could alleviate China's air pollution woes.

Are dams a better alternative than coal and nuclear energy? Are there other alternatives that are better still?

In the meantime, it was the U.S. that pioneered dam building.

The U.S. has probably also done more to encourage pollution in other countries than China has as well. Pound for pound, the U.S. is a bigger cause of climate change.

China is the source of more greenhouse gas emissions than any other country. However, the U.S., which has a much smaller population, is a very close second. In fact, China ranks seventh in terms of greenhouse gas emissions per capita, compared to second place for the U.S. Qatar, in first place, is relatively insignificant, given its small size.

Carbon dioxide added to the atmosphere can stay there for centuries. That makes historical greenhouse gas emissions an important part of the equation, and the U.S. has a huge lead on China.

In plain English, we appear to be caught in the middle of a clusterfuck.

Let's hope China's citizens can develop and maintain a better environmental ethic than their American counterparts. There's also some hope that China might be able to harness its technological prowess to seek ways to live in greater harmony with the environment.

EILEEN GU

"**P**lease believe in THE POWER OF ONE. One person can make an enormous difference in the world. One person—actually, one idea—can start a war, or end one, or subvert an entire power structure. One discovery can cure a disease or spawn new technology to benefit or annihilate the human race. You as ONE individual can change millions of lives. Think big. Do not limit your vision and do not ever compromise your dreams or ideals."

Those inspirational words are the legacy of Iris Chang, who has long been my biggest hero of Chinese ancestry. Like me, Chang was a political activist and maybe a bit of a conspiracy theorist. Her tragic death was very conspiratorial. Chang was widely mourned in China, where she gained fame as the author of *The Rape of Nanking*.

I now have a new Chinese hero, Eileen Gu.

Like Chang, Gu is Chinese-American. She has also transformed herself into a powerful political force, though she ironically shies away from politics ... sort of.

The timing is amazing. When I first published this book near the end of January 2022, I had but a vague awareness of Gu. I remember reading about some Chinese-American woman from California who was a wizard on the ski slopes. End of story.

Less than a week later, I began seeing headlines about a U.S. citizen who was a gold medal favorite—and she was competing for China! Dubbed the "Snow Princess," Gu won her first gold medal after a gutsy performance on February 8, after which her fans broke the Internet and her muddled enemies embarked on a massive orgy of impotent rage.

How could I miss such a sensational story by just two weeks? Obviously, I had to revise my book.

BIRTH OF A DREAM

ONE HAS TO WONDER if Eileen Gu is channeling Chang. At the age of 18, she wasn't just a celebrity athlete; she was also the biggest star of the 2022 Winter Olympics. She was also worth millions of dollars, which only added to the right-wingers' hypocritical attacks on her.

There are two reasons I admire Gu.

First, you have to respect her intelligence and raw talent. Unlike the army of media whores who demonize her, she has won Olympic gold. She's also a fashion model and a musician. She's bilingual. She's a pretty impressive speaker, too, and she can even handle herself in the political arena. (I loved it when she described her critics as un-educated haters who will never win a gold medal in the Olympics!)

Second, Gu isn't one of the sheeple.

Most Americans are frankly brain-dead. They obediently follow orders, wait in line and kiss the hand that stabs them in the back 24/7.

Gu, on the other hand, gave the whole world the middle finger (figuratively speaking) and charted her own course. She decided she was going to represent China in the Olympics, and that's that.

Gu announced her fateful decision on Instagram on June 6, 2019.

"I have decided to compete for China in the upcoming 2022 Winter Olympics. This was an incredibly tough decision for me to make. I am especially thankful for U.S. Ski & Snowboard (@usfreeskiteam) and the Chinese Ski Association for having the vision and belief in me to make my dreams come true. I am proud of my heritage, and equally proud of my American upbringings. The opportunity to help inspire millions of young people where my mom was born, during the 2022 Beijing Winter Olympic games is a once-in-a-lifetime opportunity to help promote the sport I love. Through skiing, I hope to unite people, promote common understanding, create communication, and forge friendships between nations. If I can help to inspire one young girl to break a boundary, my wishes will have come true."

RIGHT-WING HATE FEST

I WAS SCARCELY AWARE of Gu's existence until the 2022 Winter Olympics began. Suddenly, she was in the headlines, which were a mixture of adulation and revulsion.

From the disgruntled fans section came the articles "Olympics Jerk Watch: The American Skier Who Chose to Represent China" (Justin Peters, Slate, Feb. 6, 2022) and "Why Eileen Gu is worthy of oblivion" (Christine Flowers, *Daily Times*).

Peters tried to soften his attack by suggesting that Gu isn't a mature adult and may therefore deserve a little slack. Flowers, on the other hand, says Gu's youth and cultural heritage are no excuse.

Flowers is an attorney who has spent over two decades of her sleazy life working with immigrants who have "literally risked life and limb," crossing mountains and deserts, to come to this spectacularly wonderful country we call the United States, and none of them win gold medals for China. Why Gu can't join all the other immigrants who are mired in poverty is something Flowers can't understand.

On a more humorous note, Flowers invokes Jesse Owens, the black track star who supposedly humiliated Adolf Hitler at the 1936 Olympics in Berlin.

Contrary to the mainstream narrative, Hitler did not snub Owens. He actually congratulated him; Owens said it was the proudest moment of his life.

Owens was, however, snubbed by another leader—pResident Franklin D. Roosevelt. So who was the real racist, Adolf Hitler or FDR?

In the February 8 issue of *Sports Illustrated*, Michael Rosenberg wrote "Gu got her gold medal and China got its pawn" ("Eileen Gu's Olympic Gold for China Thrust Her Citizenship Status Into the Spotlight"). So sleazy is Eileen Gu, Rosenberg couldn't even comprehend why her first gold medal performance was observed and applauded by Thomas Bach, president of the International Olympic Committee (IOC). What kind of IOC president watches Olympic athletes perform, damn it?!

This wretched monument to stupidity appeared in *Sports Illustrated*, the magazine that thrills the world with its annual Swimsuit Issue!

USA Today unleashed Dan Wolken on Eileen Gu ("Eileen Gu's life gets more complicated after winning gold at Olympics for China," Feb. 8, 2022).

And how could that weasel-eyed whore of whores, Ben Shapiro, miss out on the action? He conveyed his regards on Facebook on February 7:

> **"Eileen Gu should leave the U.S., go live in China, and report back to us the many marvels and wonders of living under an oppressive, authoritarian regime."**

However, the most publicized attack was probably the video

starring Fox News' Tucker Carlson and Will Cain ("This is about something much bigger than Eileen Gu: Cain," Feb. 2, 2022). Cain—a recipient of The Breakfast Club's *Donkey of the Day* award—reportedly made a lot of enemies in China.

Another bottom feeder who deserves an honorable mention is Bill Maher.

The courageous Nikki Haley waited until after Gu won her third medal before she weighed in. As reported in the article "'Pick a Side': Nikki Haley's Stern Warning for American Competing for China" (Megan Turner, OutKick), the former U.S. ambassador to the United Nations said "you're standing for freedom or you're standing for human rights abuses" (for choosing to represent China over the United States).

Sadly, Haley won't win any gold medals for her amateur act. Don't her words sound eerily similar to former pResident George W. Bush's angry challenge that you're either with THEM (terrorists) or US (the U.S.)?

Bush and Haley both spat out textbook examples of a fallacy variously called a dilemma, false dilemma or false dichotomy. It is the claim that a person must make one of two choices, especially when both are unpleasant. More intelligent people who are impaled on "the horns of a dilemma" may realize that there are other choices that are being studiously ignored by the propagandist.

However, Bush and Haley both went beyond a simple dilemma. They also falsely cast the U.S. and China as symbols of good and evil, respectively. The U.S. has shown far more scorn for human rights, both domestically and in the international arena, than China.

THE LOGIC OF BLIND HATE

So why do so many Americans, particularly right-wingers (a category that today includes many Americans who think they're liberals) and media whores, hate Eileen Gu? What was her crime?

If we wade through all the ranting, Gu's critics—the ignorant masses who will never compete in the Olympics—appear to have four primary gripes.

HORNS OF A *FALSE* DILEMMA

First, they think it's inappropriate for a person who was born, raised, educated and trained in the U.S. to represent another country in the Olympics.

Second, they think something fishy is going on regarding Gu's citizenship status. You see, China doesn't allow its citizens to have dual citizenship. So did Gu give up her U.S. citizenship, or did China's government allow her to play by different rules? Gu snubbed media whores who asked that question.

Third, the angry losers crowd think it's disgusting that any athlete would represent a country with as many gross human rights violations as China.

Finally, some people think Gu's real goal is—gasp!—to earn lots of money.

Let's take a closer look at those charges.

1. Gu represented another country.

2. Gu's citizenship status is as mysterious as Obama's.

3. China is an evil empire.

4. Gu just wanted to make lots of money.

1. GU REPRESENTED ANOTHER COUNTRY

The first complaint isn't entirely true. Yes, Gu was born in the U.S. However, her mother is Chinese, she speaks fluent Chinese, and she actually spent much of her youth in China. (By the way, does anyone know where Obama was born?)

In fact, Gu says she had visited China every year since she was two years old.

Another interesting thing is Eileen's last name—Gu—and the apparent absence of her father in her life. That speaks volumes.

It also raises an interesting question: *Does citizenship trump culture?*

Many people become naturalized citizens of one country or another as part of their journey through life, but they may retain a deep connection to their ancestral homeland.

Eileen Gu is multicultural. She's also a free moral agent; her culture(s), her choice.

2. CITIZENSHIP STATUS

Regarding Gu's citizenship status, who cares? If she renounced her U.S citizenship, then she's now a Chinese citizen, which makes all four complaints moot.

If, on the other hand, China's government is bending the law to allow her to represent China, so what? The law is continuously bent and broken in the U.S., often for nefarious purposes.

In 1963, the U.S. government gave honorary citizenship status to one of history's biggest racists and warmongers, Winston Churchill. And what about all the U.S. politicians who are joined at the hip with Israel? Why do so few people question *their* loyalty?

But what about Gu's refusal to answer media whores' questions about her citizenship?

Again, so what? They're media whores. They should get down on their hands and knees and thank God that Gu even deigns to talk to them.

I quickly learned to snub media whores after I became a political activist. They're nothing but slimy liars.

3. CHINA: EVIL EMPIRE?

China vs Human Rights is a more complex issue.

I'm all for snubbing or boycotting strikingly corrupt entities. I despise entertainers who perform in Israel, for example.

But China isn't Israel. Israel's ongoing slaughter of Palestinians is a textbook example of genocide, but I've seen no convincing evidence of genocide in Xinjiang, China. As for the decline of democracy in Hong Kong, let me know when it's as far gone as Seattle or Saipan.

ANYONE INTERESTED IN STUDYING GENOCIDE SHOULD TAKE A LOOK AT IRAQ, AFGHANISTAN, LIBYA, SYRIA, AND ISRAEL.

Ironically, the United States' record on human rights is far more dismal than China's. Every U.S. athlete who competes in the Olympics has more shame to bear than Eileen Gu.

4. MONEY!

But what about complaint #4, money?

This one really isn't hard to figure out; just put yourself in Eileen Gu's shoes: you're an 18-year-old athlete performing in your first Olympics in a sport that's quite dangerous. There's a fine line between winning a gold medal versus a far less valuable silver medal. And is there a person on the planet who gives a damn about bronze?

One false move or freak accident, and Gu could have been injured, perhaps permanently, ending her career.

In addition, Gu's twin careers—skiing and modeling—are both youth-oriented. She probably won't be doing either when she's 40. The end of the road could even come at age 30.

In the meantime, Gu has a superstar status that makes her a super hot commodity. She's worth millions of dollars. For now.

If you had just one fleeting chance to make millions of dollars, what would you do?

Most Americans would sell their soul. Just look at all those overpaid media whores who get paid to slime people like Gu.

Gu is frankly a saint compared to any media whore.

If you stop and think about it, few of us are really clean.

I've earned money by working for the Seattle School District, the U.S. Postal Service and United Parcel Service, none of which I would describe as honorable. But I have to pay the rent, and it's hard finding employers that are a class act.

If I had Gu's talent, I would be a free agent, too. And if I could rake in millions of dollars before my twentieth birthday, I'd be sorely tempted, though I wouldn't sell my soul. And I certainly don't think Gu has sold her soul, either.

REALITY CHECK

IF 1) OTHER U.S. citizens are winning Olympic gold for countries other than the U.S., 2) the U.S. is far more evil than China, and 3) we grant Gu the right to capitalize on her talents and earn a lot of money, then what is the real reason America's trailer park trash hate Eileen Gu?

The answer is right under your nose: She's so damn hot!

Gu is idolized by millions of people around the world, and she helps broadcast the fact that China isn't nearly as bad a place as the U.S. Chamber of Commerce would have us believe. At the same time, Gu can earn China gold medals at America's expense.

And that's what the Olympics are really all about for Team USA.

Did you know that the U.S. is the only country that doesn't dip its national flag in honor of the host nation during the opening ceremonies of Olympic tournaments? How's that for arrogance? It might make one question all the hot air about sportsmanship and international goodwill.

No, the Olympics is just one big ego binge for the U.S., which almost always wins more medals (and more gold medals) than any other country, making it look like a really cool country.

America's media whores may also be overacting out of frustration.

I mean, the mere idea of an army of media whores launching a hate campaign against a clean cut teenaged athlete is a little gruesome, right? And what can a media whore who has done his patriotic duty by sliming Eileen Gu say when she counterattacks by winning a gold medal?

EILEEN GU WAS ACTUALLY VINDICATED BY THE TIDAL WAVE OF HATE SHE RECEIVED FROM AN ARMY OF AMERICAN TRAILER PARK TRASH.

In summary, if all those uneducated media whores aren't whining about other athletes who perform for countries other than their birth countries, then they obviously hate Eileen Gu for the simple reason that she's so damn hot. Ironically, their hypocritical, unhinged hatred vindicates her; their demonization may actually make her stronger.

At the same time, the media whores are making themselves look like the foolish scumbags they are. Collectively, they look like a one-legged man in a butt-kicking contest. Step right up to the Greatest Show on Earth, folks!

In the meantime, Eileen Gu is the perfect mascot for China, the quiet country that came out of nowhere and is suddenly kicking America's ass on all fronts. But can she represent the U.S. at the same time?

Why not?

For me, Gu is a welcome reminder that, even if 95% of Americans are brain-dead losers—thanks largely to the media whores and crappy public schools that brainwash them—there are still a few intelligent citizens out there.

And if those more mature citizens want to occasionally escape America's giddy corruption and arrogance with a sojourn in their mother country, good for them!

Before I finished this chapter, Gu won two more medals, a silver and a gold, knocking her media critics down another couple of pegs.

CONSPIRACY CORNER

As the author of *Conspiracy Science*, I have a special interest in... well, conspiracy.

Iris Chang's tragic death is shrouded in conspiracy, and Eileen Gu may be in the conspiracy zone as well.

If you've followed the headlines, you know that Gu is very close to her mother, but the media say almost nothing about her father. We're told that he graduated from Harvard, but how is it possible that no one knows his name?

If Eileen Gu doesn't want to talk about her father, that's her business. However, there are millions of people who are interested in her life story. There's also an army of media whores who would like to examine every facet of her life in their insatiable search for anything that might be embarrassing or compromising.

Surely her father's name is listed on a marriage and birth certificate—unless her parents were never married. However, even if they were never married, their relationship must have been known within their social circle. Why the secrecy? How is it possible to know the name of the school he graduated from but not his name?

I don't know what to make of it, but I smell a conspiracy.

UKRAINE

How can I write a book like this without mentioning the war in Ukraine?

Yes, Ukraine is far from China, but it is a member of China's belt and road initiative. Ukraine has been invaded by Russia, which is supposedly China's ally.

The biggest European war since World War II, the Russian-Ukrainian War has been manipulated to demonize China, similar to the coronavirus pandemic.

So, what's going on? Why did Russia invade Ukraine? How has the war affected the ties between China and Russia? How has it affected China itself? Will the war, as some observers insinuate, either persuade or dissuade China from attacking Taiwan?

My views are as provocative as they are unique. Merely mentioning them in this book would get this book banned. Therefore, you can read all about the Ukraine quagmire in this book's sequel, which should be published in early 2023. Learn more at ChinaWatch.pro.

SUMMARY

And so we reach the end of my interpretation of the global duel between China and the U.S. What do you think?

I'm certainly willing to admit that I don't know everything, and I can't predict the future. My book doubtless includes some errors or bad judgments.

On the other hand, I think my perspective is far more accurate (and ethical) than the river of bullshit that's gushed by Western media whores 24/7.

In summary, I see China and the U.S. as very similar yet very different at the same time.

They rank as the third and fourth biggest countries in the world, and each one is a commercial power house that scares the hell out of environmentalists. They both have enormous populations, with China ranked #1 in the world and the U.S. #3, with about one quarter China's population.

On the positive side, China has a far better track record than the U.S. It did not have a reputation as an empire builder even in ancient times. China hasn't fought a war since 1979. Before that, it fought defensive wars during World War II and the Korean War.

China's bankers don't have the same reputation as Wall Street for screwing other countries.

China doesn't have the same reputation as the U.S. for screwing its own citizens and consumers around the world. China offers its citizens free health care and has done more to fight poverty than the U.S. has. Lacking the United States' economic and political clout and reputation for thuggery, China has little choice but to play fair if it wants to do business with other countries.

Nevertheless, China's history and political geography are far more complex than the United States', dumping some major headaches in its lap. China could even be said to be a victim of geography, as it is partially blocked by a string of islands largely controlled by the U.S.

And so, China's government is widely criticized for its policies in Tibet, Xinjiang and Hong Kong, along with its desire for reunification with Taiwan. The South China Sea is another thorny problem. The U.S. government also continues to blame the coronavirus pandemic on China. China has long been accused of stealing technology and failing to follow the very "international rule of law" the U.S. so shamefully manipulates.

If we can judge by trends, China would appear to be the winner. It has been steadily growing in power since the 1970's, and its very rate of growth has accelerated in recent years. China now has the world's second biggest economy and third most powerful military. Its economy is predicted to eclipse the U.S. within about a decade. Some observers already describe the U.S. as a Chinese colony.

Exactly when China will achieve military parity is harder to say, but it is already a leader in several key areas, including hypersonic missiles. It also has more ships than the U.S. Navy.

At the same time, there are increasing signs that the United States is in decline. The caliber of our leaders is frankly shocking, and they seem more interested in helping Israel than their own country. An army of homeless people in liberal Seattle and San Francisco makes one wonder if there's any hope.

On the international stage, the United States' clumsy retreat from Afghanistan after a pointless invasion and two-decade occupation has made it the world's laughingstock.

Perhaps the most exciting thing the Western media are ignoring is the fact that China represents a challenge not just to U.S. supremacy but also to the white power establishment in general.

Centuries ago, the North African city of Carthage was a major power that challenged Rome. Later, the Mongols conquered most of Eurasia.

However, white people have effectively ruled the world for more than 500 years. China is now poised to upset the apple cart, and that could usher in a new era of freedom for people around the world, notably the Muslim arc, Africa and Latin America.

In the end, we obviously have to acknowledge the fact that China isn't perfect. Moreover, it's entirely possible that the human race has gone so far down the road of no return that there's no hope.

But what's the use of living without hope?

We should always cling to hope. More importantly, we should get involved and do what we can to make the world a better place.

In that spirit, I say Viva China! I trust you far more than I trust my own country, and I think you're doing some wonderful things.

I hope you can manage to peacefully bring Taiwan back into the fold, and I wish all the people of China peace, prosperity and happiness.

APPENDIX

RECORDS & ACCOMPLISHMENTS

LONGEST WALL

Of course, it could only be the fabled Great Wall of China, which stretches for 2,150 miles. Hardier tourists can explore the branches and spurs that stretch on for another 2,193 miles. *Source: "10 Guinness World Records Held by China" (TravelQuest)*

LARGEST PALACE

It took three architects and one million workers to build China's Imperial Palace in Beijing in the 15th century. It includes 980 different buildings and nearly 9,000 rooms sprawling over 178 acres. *Source: "10 Guinness World Records Held by China" (TravelQuest)*

TALLEST BUILDINGS

Of the ten tallest buildings in the world, those ranking #3, #5 and #8-10 are in China. China's tallest building is the Shanghai Tower, which measures 2,073 feet (632 m). It is home to the world's tallest hotel, the J Hotel, as well as the fastest elevator. Guangzhou's CTF Tower—which ties another Chinese skyscraper for 8th/9th place—is also the highest terracotta building in the world. It's just thirty-seven feet shorter than the United States' tallest building, the One World Trade Center. *Source: "List of tallest buildings" (Wikipedia)*

TALLEST OUTDOOR ELEVATOR

Built into the side of a quartzite cliff, the Bailong Elevator in Zhangjiajie National Forest Park, Hunan, reaches a height of 1,069 feet (326 m). A journey of just under two minutes rewards passengers with breathtaking views of karst monoliths below. *Source: "Shanghai Tower picks up 3 Guinness World Records including fastest elevator," Jenni Marsh and Jane Sit, CNN, April 19, 2017*

LONGEST BRIDGE

Completed in 2010, China's Danyang-Kunshan Grand Bridge spans a breathtaking 102 miles. It runs between Shanghai and Nanjing in the Jiangsu province, carrying the Beijing-Shanghai High-Speed Railway across the Yangtze River delta, from Danyang to Kunshan. In fact, China boasts the five longest bridges in the world, along with the seventh and ninth longest. *Source: "The Ten Longest Bridges on Earth"*

LONGEST BRIDGE SPANNING OPEN SEA

The Hangzhou Bay Bridge carries traffic over 22 miles (36 km) of open sea to connect the two coastal cities of Ningbo and Jiaxing. *Source: "China Pride," Jonathan Clements,* The Times

HIGHEST ARCH BRIDGE

Passengers riding the Lhasa-Nyingchi bullet train to Tibet pass through 47 tunnels and 121 bridges, including the Zangmu Railway Bridge, the world's largest and highest arch bridge. The bridge stands at an altitude of nearly 11,000 feet (3,350 m). *Source: "Biggest, tallest and fastest: China's record-breaking attractions" (Travel Asia Weekly, July 2, 2021)*

FASTEST TRAIN

China boasts the fastest and second fastest trains in the world. The fastest is the Shanghai Maglev, which zips across the country at a blistering 286 miles per hour (460 kph). It is also the only train in the world that uses magnetic levitation (Maglev) rather than conventional wheels on steel rails. As a bonus, the ride is said to be super smooth. The fastest train in the U.S. is the Acela, which can reach speeds of 150 mph. *Source: "Flying without wings: The world's fastest trains" (Ben Jones, CNN, Dec. 10, 2021)*

LARGEST HIGH-SPEED RAIL NETWORK

In early 2017, China's high-speed rail network measured 12,427 miles. Another 9,320 miles is scheduled to be added by 2025. *Source: "10 Guinness World Records Held by China" (TravelQuest)*

LONGEST MONORAIL

Opened in 2011, Line 3 of the Chongqing Rail Transit system has since been extended to 41 miles (67 km). *Source: "China Pride,"* Jonathan Clements, The Times

LARGEST SCIENCE MUSEUM

Opened in 2008, the Guangdong Science Centre covers approximately .2 square miles (450,000 m2). The museum resembles a kapok flower from above, while its flanks suggest "ships sailing into the future." *Source: "China Pride,"* Jonathan Clements, The Times

LARGEST GROUP OF LIFE-SIZED STATUES

One of the greatest archaeological discoveries of the 20th century was a vast assemblage of life-size terracotta warriors and horses in the tomb of China's first emperor, Qin Shihuang. Discovered in 1974, the now famous Terracotta Army is just a portion of the treasures waiting to be discovered in the vast tomb. *Source: "China Pride,"* Jonathan Clements, The Times

TALLEST STONE BUDDHA

There are bigger Buddhas made of more modern materials, but the

Giant Buddha of Leshan, in Sichuan province, is the biggest stone Buddha, at 232 feet (71 m). In fact, it is the largest pre-modern statue in the world. *Source: "China Pride," Jonathan Clements,* The Times

LARGEST PRODUCER OF ENERGY

Most of China's energy was produced from burning coal when the record was made official in 2016. However, China is investing heavily in sustainable energy sources and is now the largest producer of solar panels, wind turbines and lithium-ion batteries. *Source: "10 Guinness World Records Held by China" (TravelQuest)*

HIGHEST VINEYARD

The Pure Land & Super-High Altitude Vineyard in Lhasa, Tibet, is 11,689 feet (3,563 m) above sea level.

Even without this high-altitude vineyard, China would still rank second behind Spain in terms of vineyard area. China is also second among countries in wine consumption, surpassed only by the U.S. *Source: "10 Guinness World Records Held by China" (TravelQuest)*

LARGEST ONLINE SHOPPING BONANZA

Who knew a campus celebration for singles would become the world's largest online shopping bonanza? On November 11, 2014, commercial titan Alibaba pocketed $8.9 billion in 24 hours. In 2021, Alibaba raked in $84.5 billion. *Source: "China Pride," Jonathan Clements,* The Times

COMPARISONS

Various Comparisons	China	U.S.
Population (2021)	1.4 billion	333 million
Ave. Life Expectancy (2019)	77.3 years	78.8 years
Free health care?	Yes	No
Crime Rate (2021)	30.14	47.81
> Rank	109	56
GDP (2020)*	$14.7 T	$20.9 T
GDP Per Capita (2020)	$10,434	$63,413
National Debt (2021)	~$5.7 T	~$29.6 T
Incarceration Rate Per 100,000 Citizens	121	639
CO2 Emissions (million tons)	11680.42	4535.30
CO2 Emissions Per Capita (tons)	8.2	13.68
> Rank	13th	28th

*BEAR IN MIND THAT GDP PER CAPITA FIGURES FOR THE U.S. ARE SKEWED BY THE SUPER RICH. WE HAVE MORE BILLIONAIRES PER CAPITA THAN CHINA, AND WE ALSO HAVE RICHER BILLIONAIRES.

SOURCES:

Life Expectancy—Gap in life expectancy between China and US tells different social ideals," Hu Naijun, Global Times, Dec. 29, 2021

Crime Rate—World Population Review

GDP—Investopedia

GDP Per Capita—World Bank

National Debt—Chinas' National Debt Clock / U.S. National Debt Clock

Incarceration Rate—Wikipedia

CO2 Emissions—World Population Review

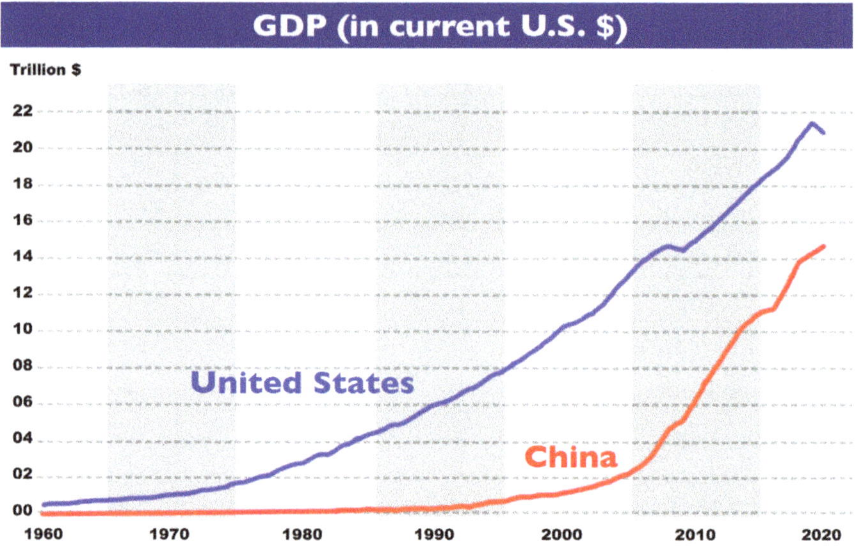

GDP Per Capita	China	U.S.
1976	$141	$20,747
1989	$383	$28,098
2021	$8,840	$56,200

Coronavirus: Pandemic vs Plandemic (Jan. 2022)	
China	**U.S.**
Fewer than 5,000 deaths due to pandemic	Nearly 900,000 deaths due to pandemic
Hubei the only province to experience major outbreak	Every state has suffered multiple major outbreaks.
Very few people suffering with Long Covid	Epidemic of Long Covid affecting millions
Citizens are able to live normal lives.	Elderly and vulnerable people still have to limit social contact.
63% of population fully vaccinated	87% of population fully vaccinated
Exported over 2 million vaccine doses, prioritizing Global South	Hoarded vaccines
Poverty alleviation programs continues uninterrupted	Millions have fallen deeper into poverty
Google, Facebook and Twitter banned in China	Google and popular social networks appointed themselves guardians of the truth.

ONLINE RESOURCES:

"China vs United States" (omni index)

"Country Comparison" (WorldData.info)

"Country Comparison" (countryeconomy.com)

"Military Power of USA & China"

"Comparison of China and United States Military Strengths (2022)" (Global Firepower)

"Military Stats" (NationMaster)

"An Interactive Look at the U.S.-China Military Scorecard" (RAND)

TIMELINE

1592 - Japan invades Korea with the intent of taking China.

1787 - France invades and takes control of Vietnam, which borders China.

1839 - Great Britain attacks China in the first Opium War.

1856 - Great Britain attacks China in the second Opium War.

1889 - Eleven countries, including the U.S., invade China to put down the Boxer Rebellion.

1894 - Japan invades Korea for a second time. It also takes the island of Taiwan, with the ultimate goal of taking all of China.

1898 - The U.S. launches the Spanish-American War, a war of imperialism, making the Philippines one of its colonies.

1912 - 2,000 years of imperial rule end as China declares itself a republic with Sun Yat-sen its first president.

1927 - A civil war pitting the Kuomintang (Chinese nationalists) against the Communists begins. It will last intermittently until 1949.

1931 - Japan invades China in a war that will kill over 22 million civilians. (Some people regard this as the true beginning of World War II.)

1945 - The Potsdam Declaration requires Japan to return all territories stolen from China, including Taiwan.

1949 - Mao Zedong proclaims the establishment of the People's Republic of China.

1950 - The U.S. invades Korea and considers pushing on into China.

1953 - Mao Zedong begins rural collectivization based on a five-year plan. Individual land ownership is abolished and replaced with cooperatives.

1955 - The U.S. invades Vietnam.

1958 - Mao Zedong's "Great Leap Forward" begins.

1959 - China's Great Famine begins, killing an estimated 15-55 million people. Commonly blamed on Mao Zedong's Great Leap Forward, it lasts into 1961.

1966 - Mao Zedong launches his disastrous "Cultural Revolution," in which "Red Guards" search for and destroy anything considered bourgeois or Western. Millions of people are killed, and much of China's cultural heritage is destroyed.

1971 - China joins the United Nations as the People's Republic of China is recognized as China's legitimate government.

1972 - U.S. pResident Richard Nixon visits China, normalizing relations between the two countries.

1978 - Deng Xiaoping becomes China's supreme leader. He will steer the country away from communism, earning the nickname the "Architect of Modern China."

1979 - China's "One-Child Policy" is introduced as the population reaches 900 million.

1987 - Huawei Technologies Co., Ltd. is founded. It will evolve into one of the world's biggest tech firms. Western-style fast food is introduced as Kentucky Fried Chicken opens its first store in China.

1989 - Tiananmen Square Protests pit student protesters against the government.

1992 - In what will become known as the 1992 Consensus,

representatives from the PRC and ROC (mainland China and Taiwan) agree that there is only one sovereign state encompassing both mainland China and Taiwan, but disagree about which of the two governments is the legitimate government of this state.

1997 - China takes control of Hong Kong's sovereignty.

2001 - China is admitted to the World Trade Organization (WTO). A U.S. EP-3 spy plane collides with a Chinese fighter jet 70 miles off the coast of the Chinese island of Hainan.

2002 - Poverty is reduced to 88 million from 490 million in 1981.

2007 - China's GDP growth is a staggering 14.2%. After being refused port in Hong Kong, a U.S. naval fleet transits the Taiwan Straits, within 100 miles of the coast of China.

2008 - The XXIX Summer Olympics are held in Beijing.

2010 - China surpasses Japan as the second largest economy.

2012 - China becomes the largest trading nation in the world.

2013 - China launches an ambitious Belt and Road Initiative (BRI), which will involve building infrastructure in countries around the world. It is scheduled for completion by 2049.

2018 - The Pentagon bans the sale of Huawei and ZTE phones on U.S. military bases. Huawei CFO Meng Wanzhou is arrested in Canada at the request of the U.S. government on charges that she violated U.S. sanctions against Iran. Huawei knocks off Apple to become the second biggest smart phone vendor in the world.

2019 - pResident Donald Trump effectively bans Huawei from the U.S. with a national security order.

2020 - A coronavirus pandemic begins. The U.S. is quick to blame it on China, ignoring provocative evidence implicating Fort

Detrick, Maryland. Huawei becomes the world's most popular smart phone maker in spite of U.S. sanctions.

2021 - A global computer chip shortage erupts, apparently caused largely by the U.S. government's reckless anti-China sanctions. CFO Meng Wanzhou returns to a hero's welcome after being released.

SOME ONLINE TIMELINES

"China Timeline" (History.com)

"The People's Republic of China: 70 Years of Economic History" (Iman Ghosh, Visual Capitalist, Oct. 12, 2019)

"Huawei Ban Timeline" (Sean Keane, c/net, Sept. 30, 2021)

BELT AND ROAD INITIATIVE MEMBERS

As of December 2021, 144 countries have joined the Belt and Road Initiative (BRI) by signing a Memorandum of Understanding (MoU) with China. I prepared two lists of the BRI members, an alphabetical list and a list arranged by region.

Seven countries (Austria, Benin, Comoros, Congo D.R., Dominica, Niger and Russia) are marked with asterisks because of some confusion regarding their status. Independent information confirming their status as BRI members is either lacking or contradictory.

Note the following regional abbreviations: Eurasia (countries lying partly in Europe and partly in Asia), Mideast (Middle East), Carib (Caribbean), CAm (Central America), SAm (South America), PacificO (PacificOcean), IndianO (IndianOcean).

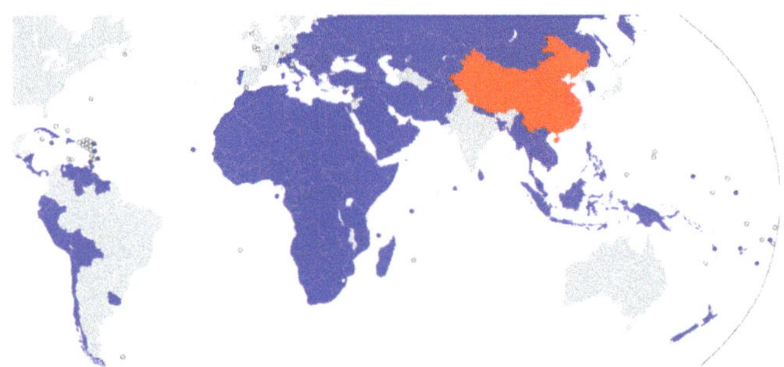

THE U.S. AND ITS ALLIES LOOK AWFUL LONELY ON THIS MAP, WHICH ILLUSTRATES COUNTRIES THAT HAVE JOINED THE BRI. (SEE CREDITS)

Below are links to a few websites that appear to have some fairly good information about countries belonging to the BRI.

- "Green Finance & Development Center" (greenfdc.org/countries-of-the-belt-and-road-initiative-bri)
- "LehmanBrown" (www.lehmanbrown.com/insights-newsletter/belt-road-initiative/)
- "Belt and Road Tracker" (www.cfr.org/article/belt-and-road-tracker)
- "Belt and Road Initiative" (Wikipedia) (en.wikipedia.org/wiki/Belt_and_Road_Initiative)

NOTE: IN THE TABLES BELOW, AN ASTERISK (*) DENOTES SOME UNCERTAINTY REGARDING A COUNTRY'S STATUS AS A BRI MEMBER, GENERALLY DUE TO A LACK OF OFFICIAL RECORDS.

BRI: Alphabetical List

Country		Country	
Afghanistan	Asia	Lithuania	Europe
Albania	Europe	Luxembourg	Europe
Algeria	Africa	Madagascar	IndianO
Angola	Africa	Malaysia	Asia
Antigua and Barbuda	Carib	Maldives	IndianO
Armenia	Asia	Mali	Africa
Austria*	Europe	Malta	Europe
Azerbaijan	Eurasia	Mauritania	Africa
Bahrain	Mideast	Micronesia, Fed. Sts.	PacificO
Bangladesh	Asia	Moldova	Europe
Barbados	Carib	Mongolia	Asia
Belarus	Europe	Montenegro	Europe
Benin*	Africa	Morocco	Africa
Bolivia	SAm	Mozambique	Africa
Bosnia and Herzegovina	Europe	Myanmar	Asia
Botswana	Africa	Namibia	Africa
Brunei Darussalam	Asia	Nepal	Asia
Bulgaria	Europe	New Zealand	PacificO
Burundi	Africa	Nicaragua	CAm
Cabo Verde	Africa	Niger*	Africa
Cambodia	Asia	Nigeria	Africa
Cameroon	Africa	Niue	PacificO
Chad	Africa	North Macedonia	Europe
Chile	SAm	Oman	Mideast
China	Asia	Pakistan	Asia
Comoros*	IndianO	Panama	CAm
Congo, Dem. Rep.	Africa	Papua New Guinea	PacificO
Congo, Rep.*	Africa	Peru	SAm
Cook Islands	PacificO	Philippines	Asia
Costa Rica	CAm	Poland	Europe
Côte d'Ivoire	Africa	Portugal	Europe
Croatia	Europe	Qatar	Mideast
Cuba	Carib	Romania	Europe
Cyprus	Europe	Russian Federation*	Eurasia
Czech Republic	Europe	Rwanda	Africa
Djibouti	Africa	Samoa	PacificO
Dominica*	Carib	Saudi Arabia	Mideast
Dominican Republic	Carib	Senegal	Africa
Ecuador	SAm	Serbia	Europe
Egypt, Arab Rep.	Africa	Seychelles	IndianO
El Salvador	CAm	Sierra Leone	Africa
Equatorial Guinea	Africa	Singapore	Asia
Eritrea	Africa	Slovak Republic	Europe
Estonia	Europe	Slovenia	Europe
Ethiopia	Africa	Solomon Islands	PacificO
Fiji	PacificO	Somalia	Africa
Gabon	Africa	South Africa	Africa
Gambia, The	Africa	South Sudan	Africa
Georgia	Eurasia	Sri Lanka	Asia
Ghana	Africa	Sudan	Africa
Greece	Europe	Suriname	SAm
Grenada	Carib	Syrian Arab Republic	Mideast
Guinea	Africa	Tajikistan	Asia
Guinea-Bissau	Africa	Tanzania	Africa
Guyana	SAm	Thailand	Asia
Hungary	Europe	Timor-Leste	PacificO
Indonesia	Asia	Togo	Africa
Iran, Islamic Rep.	Asia	Tonga	PacificO

BRI: Alphabetical List			
Country		**Country**	
Iraq	Mideast	Trinidad and Tobago	Carib
Italy	Europe	Tunisia	Africa
Jamaica	Carib	Turkey	Eurasia
Kazakhstan	Asia	Uganda	Africa
Kenya	Africa	Ukraine	Europe
Kiribati	PacificO	United Arab Emirates	Mideast
Korea, Rep.	Asia	Uruguay	SAm
Kuwait	Mideast	Uzbekistan	Asia
Kyrgyz Republic	Asia	Vanuatu	PacificO
Lao PDR	Asia	Venezuela, RB	SAm
Latvia	Europe	Vietnam	Asia
Lebanon	Mideast	Yemen, Rep.	Mideast
Lesotho	Africa	Zambia	Africa
Liberia	Africa	Zimbabwe	Africa
Libya	Africa		

BRI: Regional List			
Country		**Country**	
Afghanistan	Asia	Congo, Rep.*	Africa
Armenia	Asia	Côte d'Ivoire	Africa
Bangladesh	Asia	Djibouti	Africa
Brunei Darussalam	Asia	Egypt, Arab Rep.	Africa
Cambodia	Asia	Equatorial Guinea	Africa
China	Asia	Eritrea	Africa
Indonesia	Asia	Ethiopia	Africa
Iran, Islamic Rep.	Asia	Gabon	Africa
Kazakhstan	Asia	Gambia, The	Africa
Korea, Rep.	Asia	Ghana	Africa
Kyrgyz Republic	Asia	Guinea	Africa
Lao PDR	Asia	Guinea-Bissau	Africa
Malaysia	Asia	Kenya	Africa
Mongolia	Asia	Lesotho	Africa
Myanmar	Asia	Liberia	Africa
Nepal	Asia	Libya	Africa
Pakistan	Asia	Mali	Africa
Philippines	Asia	Mauritania	Africa
Singapore	Asia	Morocco	Africa
Sri Lanka	Asia	Mozambique	Africa
Tajikistan	Asia	Namibia	Africa
Thailand	Asia	Niger*	Africa
Uzbekistan	Asia	Nigeria	Africa
Vietnam	Asia	Rwanda	Africa
Azerbaijan	Eurasia	Senegal	Africa
Georgia	Eurasia	Sierra Leone	Africa
Russian Federation*	Eurasia	Somalia	Africa
Turkey	Eurasia	South Africa	Africa
Albania	Europe	South Sudan	Africa
Austria*	Europe	Sudan	Africa
Belarus	Europe	Tanzania	Africa
Bosnia and Herzegovina	Europe	Togo	Africa
Bulgaria	Europe	Tunisia	Africa
Croatia	Europe	Uganda	Africa
Czech Republic	Europe	Zambia	Africa
Cyprus	Europe	Zimbabwe	Africa
Estonia	Europe	Antigua and Barbuda	Carib
Greece	Europe	Barbados	Carib
Hungary	Europe	Cuba	Carib
Italy	Europe	Dominica*	Carib
Latvia	Europe	Dominican Republic	Carib
Lithuania	Europe	Grenada	Carib

BRI: Regional List			
Country		**Country**	
Luxembourg	Europe	Jamaica	Carib
Malta	Europe	Trinidad and Tobago	Carib
Moldova	Europe	Costa Rica	CAm
Montenegro	Europe	El Salvador	CAm
North Macedonia	Europe	Nicaragua	CAm
Poland	Europe	Panama	CAm
Portugal	Europe	Bolivia	SAm
Romania	Europe	Chile	SAm
Serbia	Europe	Ecuador	SAm
Slovak Republic	Europe	Guyana	SAm
Slovenia	Europe	Peru	SAm
Ukraine	Europe	Suriname	SAm
Bahrain	Mideast	Uruguay	SAm
Iraq	Mideast	Venezuela, RB	SAm
Kuwait	Mideast	Cook Islands	PacificO
Lebanon	Mideast	Fiji	PacificO
Oman	Mideast	Kiribati	PacificO
Qatar	Mideast	Micronesia, Fed. Sts.	PacificO
Saudi Arabia	Mideast	New Zealand	PacificO
Syrian Arab Republic	Mideast	Niue	PacificO
United Arab Emirates	Mideast	Papua New Guinea	PacificO
Yemen, Rep.	Mideast	Samoa	PacificO
Algeria	Africa	Solomon Islands	PacificO
Angola	Africa	Timor-Leste	PacificO
Benin*	Africa	Tonga	PacificO
Botswana	Africa	Vanuatu	PacificO
Burundi	Africa	Comoros*	IndianO
Cabo Verde	Africa	Madagascar	IndianO
Cameroon	Africa	Maldives	IndianO
Chad	Africa	Seychelles	IndianO
Congo, Dem. Rep.	Africa		

PREDICTIONS

WHAT POLITICAL BUFF DOESN'T like making predictions?

In fact, lots of people are obsessed with making predictions about China these days. After all, it's the biggest moving target in the world today, or at least the most visible. The U.S. appears to be going nowhere, but China is a country on a mission to excel.

MILITARY

Of course, one question that's on everyone's mind is war. Will China and the U.S. fight World War III? If so, who will win?

I discuss those questions in the chapter "War!"

But when will China's military be on a par with the United States'?

Some "experts" say China can't achieve parity before 2050. But exactly what do they mean by "parity"? If China wants to match the U.S. military's arsenal plane for plane, nuclear missile for nuclear missile, then it will need some time to catch up. And how could China ever hope to emulate the U.S. in establishing 500-800 military bases around the world? How could China ever hope to match a war-loving country like the U.S. in terms of experience?

I'm a big fan of asymmetrical warfare, the type of fighting that got Uncle Sam's ass kicked in Vietnam and Afghanistan, not to mention the Chosin Reservoir in Korea. I also think China has some big advantages—and the U.S. some big disadvantages—that are being omitted from the equation.

China's primary goal in the military arena has to be defense, and I think it has pretty much secured its security. Sure, the U.S. could probably still destroy China if it really wanted to, but China can destroy the U.S. in return. Suppose Team USA's vaunted overwhelming military superiority allowed it to strike China with 50 nuclear missiles, and just one Chinese nuke landed in the U.S.

Frankly, I think such a scenario would pretty much turn the U.S. into toast. Destroying China would wreck America's economy and would also be the final nail in its public image coffin. And nuking San Francisco would not be a trivial matter. Any country itching to rebel against the American Empire would be emboldened by a U.S. that would be devastated by such an exchange.

But how can China defend its overseas trading empire? Who will protect the outposts of the Belt and Road Initiative?

China's navy is already bigger than that of the United States, and it continues to build aircraft carriers, which are useful in projecting power. It has aircraft, missiles and submarines that can target the U.S. It has the ability to shoot down U.S. satellites.

China is beginning to establish military bases, including one in East Africa. It has forged an alliance with Iran that could be positively explosive.

Amazingly, almost unbelievably, the dysfunctional, militaristic U.S. still has a stable full of allies, while China seems almost alone. Nevertheless, I think China's emphasis on building bridges instead of dropping bombs is paying off. The message is slowly getting out that "Communist China" is actually a class act compared to that phony beacon of democracy, the U.S.

China has already improved millions of people's lives in Latin

America and Africa, and it is poised to replace the U.S. as the chief power broker in the Middle East. China has proved that soft power can trump hard power, and I think this strategy is going to reap even bigger dividends in the near future.

So when will China's de facto military power be equivalent to the United States'?

At the rate China's beefing up its military, I think it will be significantly stronger in 2025, and it will probably blow observers' minds in 2030. I also think China's soft power will be far greater in 2030, and its hard power and soft power combined will make it the United States' equal.

Of course, the U.S. could try something sneaky, like putting a semi-respectable pResident in office. But as long as we continue (s) electing fucktards like Donald Trump and Joe Biden, we're virtually guaranteeing our fall into obscurity.

TAIWAN

Taiwan will be reunited with China by 2030.

Will China take Taiwan back with a military assault or a blockade? Will the U.S. come to Tainwan's aid? Will we see WWIII?

I can't answer those questions. However, many observers think China has the power to retake Taiwan now, and its power will continue growing, while the U.S. may be in decline. At the same time, the United States' stupid antics and politicians (e.g. Nancy Pelosi) are only hastening the day of reckoning.

ECONOMY

Another popular question: When will China's economy be as big as America's?

In his book *Fearing China* (2015), Terry D. Wittenmyer predicted that China would have the world's biggest economy by 2024. In more recent years, people were predicting that spectacular event would happen around 2027-2028. However, others are now pushing the date up to 2033.

I'm going to go out on a limb and predict that China will be #1 in 2030. I just think China has too many pans in the fire to take lightly. At the same time, I think the U.S. is going to help by continuing to self-destruct, making it an easier target to surpass.

COMPUTER CHIPS

Will China ever be able to catch up with Taiwan in the computer chips arena?

I think the answer is yes, and I predict it will happen by 2030.

China has vast resources and a can-do attitude. It also has its back to the wall; not achieving independence in the realm of computer chips would be an enormous anchor around its neck.

The computer chip war is hard to understand, partly because of the complexity of computer chip design and manufacturing and partly because Western media whores have apparently imposed a virtual blackout on significant events in China.

However, China appears to be making significant progress. In fact, one might argue that China has two goals—1) acquire the ability to manufacture high-end silicon chips and 2) take charge of the emerging carbon-based chip industry.

I predict that China will accomplish both by 2030. I also predict that, by 2025, its progress will be sufficient to upset the industry.

Right now, Team USA has its fingers crossed, hoping that China will utterly fail in its quest for computer chip self-sufficiency. But I think that Team USA will be shitting bricks by 2025, as it becomes clear that China will soon be king of the hill.

This revelation will encourage increased foreign investment in China, and some of the key players that are currently on Team USA's side will jump ship for China, accelerating its race towards computer chip independence.

HUAWEI SMART PHONE

No quitter, Huawei released its Mate Pro 50 in 2021 as it continues searching for a way to overcome U.S. sanctions. Can Huawei hang in there, or will the Mate Pro 50 be the end of the line?

I predict that Huawei's survival will be assured by 2025. But can it ever again capture the coveted title of world's most popular smart phone?

Huawei's best publicist may be Donald Trump, who did everything he could to destroy it and has so far failed. From #1 to life support and back to #1. Sounds like a great idea for a movie, doesn't it?

Yes, I think Huawei will become #1 yet again. Once it gets back on its feet, it will be enthusiastically supported by 1.4 billion patriotic Chinese, who will catapult it onto the global stage once again. Buoyed by its too-cool operating system, Harmony, and a selection of apps that can compete with Google, I think Huawei will take charge.

My prediction: Huawei will regain the crown in 2027.

OPERATING SYSTEMS

Harmony and Euler will be offering stiff competition not just to Android but to Microsoft Windows and Apple Mac OS by 2025.

IRAN

What could be more intriguing than that exciting alliance between China and Iran?

The potential is mind-boggling, but not much has happened so far. Was it all just talk?

I predict that the alliance will bear fruit, partly because neither country really has a choice. Iran is a powerful country, but Israel is determined to destroy it, and it can certainly do a lot of damage with the support of its vassal, the U.S. China, on the other hand, would be crippled without Iran's oil, which it continues to purchase despite U.S. sanctions.

But would China go so far as to build a military base in Iran?

As I said, I'm going to go out on a limb and predict that China will build at least one military base in the country, on the east side of the Strait of Hormuz. I predict that the new base will be announced in 2023. Though it will probably begin as a port, it would almost certainly be militarized.

■ ■

Below is a summary of my predictions.

- China's hard power and soft power combined will put it on a par with the U.S. military by 2030.
- China's economy will surpass that of the United States by 2030.
- China will achieve independence in the silicon chips arena by 2030. It will become the global leader in carbon-based chips in the process.
- The Harmony and Euler operating systems will be offering stiff competition to Android, Microsoft Windows and Apple Mac OS by 2025.
- Huawei's smart phone will once again be the world's most popular cell phone in 2027.
- China will have a de facto military base in Iran by 2023, consisting of a facility on the east side of the Strait of Hormuz.

Obviously, my predictions can't all be accurate, and it's doubtful that any of them will happen on the exact dates listed. But the world will clearly be a different place in 2030. At that time, we can look back on my predictions and gauge their accuracy.

In the meantime, what are your predictions?

MORE RESOURCES

Below are links to a few online resources that appear to complement this book.

As much as I hate YouTube, which is owned by Google, it appears to have relatively good content focusing on China (along with a lot of videos that are nothing but Western propaganda). Nevertheless, take all the resources listed on this page with a grain of salt. Some of them could be slick propaganda posted by people posing as truthmongers.

1. Friends of Socialist China (Facebook) (www.facebook.com/socialistchina)

2. "How The Threat Of China Was Made In The USA" (www.youtube.com/watch?v=KuPuXAUXZjY)

3. Cyrus Janssen (www.youtube.com/results?search_query=cyrus+janssen)

4. Eyes of Real China (www.youtube.com/channel/UCnNjcEwEpTSefQuaUVA56GA)

5. Long Xin (www.youtube.com/channel/UCF9sOUJ0icAT_7i3qXQAFiA)

6. Vision of China (www.youtube.com/channel/UCm6xGHDc_Lr6uo5dMDNc-Lg)

7. China Quicktake (www.youtube.com/channel/UCC2qfhnOV6svDcXIQDDhe_A)

8. The Developing China (www.youtube.com/channel/UC_msBiJIyLDWRRU-yPuh5sQ)

9. "Why is the Caribbean Choosing China ? China Digital Currency is Changing Everything!" (www.youtube.com/watch?v=gi9iPkrsDlM&t=5s)

CREDITS

The content displayed in this book consists of text and images. If you are interested in using any content from this book in your own project, please see KPow Book's Permissions page (www.kpowbooks. com/permissions).

If you see any content that you feel is being used unfairly or illegally, please contact me @ www.kpowbooks.com/contact. (If, for some reason, you are unable to contact me, or you don't receive a response within a few days, you can also post a message in my blog.)

TEXT

All text is copyrighted by the author except for quoted material taken from other sources, all of which is duly credited.

IMAGES

A few images displayed in this book are in the public domain. However, the majority were either created by the author or purchased and licensed from commercial sources. Images used with special permission are listed below.

■ ■

A Brief History — By Officia do Palácio do Planalto - Flickr, CC BY 2.0, commons.wikimedia.org/w/index.php?curid=79804675
Note: I modified this image, erasing the background.

Chinese People — By TheDrive - This file was derived from: Gobi desert en.jpg, CC BY-SA 4.0, https://commons.wikimedia.org/w/index.php?curid=51713598
Note: I modified this image, adding the stylized people.

Hong Kong — (Hong Kong protest on right) By Studio Incendo - https://www.flickr.com/photos/studiokanu/48073669892/in/album-72157709109973522/, CC BY 2.0, https://commons.wikimedia.org/w/index.php?curid=79742972

Game of Clowns — (Volodowhore Zelensky) By President.gov.ua, CC BY 4.0, https://commons.wikimedia.org/w/index.php?curid=84298249

Huawei — By 中国新闻网, CC BY 3.0, https://commons.wikimedia.org/w/index.php?curid=110508647

Environment — By Roland Seitre - Institute of Hydrobiology, Chinese Academy of Sciences, CC BY-SA 3.0, https://commons.wikimedia.org/w/index.php?curid=95653143

Belt and Road Initiative Members — By Owennson - Own work, CC BY-SA 4.0, commons.wikimedia.org/w/index.php?curid=78386561

ABOUT THE AUTHOR

IN MY STUDIES, I'VE discovered that the overwhelming majority of authors of books about political topics have amazingly
little to say about themselves. That's probably because most
are propagandists.

As both a political activist and a student of philosophy,
I'm not afraid of shocking ideas and the naked truth. Indeed, some of my books explore issues few people would
dare mention.

However, I don't want to publish the same stuff about
myself in every book I write. Instead, you can visit my website
DavidBlomstrom.com.

In a nutshell, I was born and raised in rural West Dakota,
spent four years in the U.S. Navy, got a degree in wildlife
biology and spent about a decade working in the Alaskan
wilderness, then spent 16 years working as a teacher in Gothic

Seattle, where I had my political awakening. I quickly became a whistle-blower and a political activist, eventually running for public office ten times.

In short, I've done my homework—and I'm far from finished. (Check out my books.)

I'M WORKING ON A number of books focusing on political science and philosophy (or, as I like to call it, *politix*), philosophy and symbols of the 50 U.S. states.

The book you're reading now—*China vs USA*—was published almost simultaneously with *What Is Conspiracy?: More than a Theory*.

These are my tamest political books by far and are probably the only ones you will ever see in a boostore or library. The rest are effectively dead on arrival; they would be immediately banned. The problem is I'm too truthful, and I tackle taboo topics that other authors won't even mention.

The book you're reading now is part of a triad that includes *China Watch*, which will be published as an annual report on China's progress and the state of U.S.-China relations.

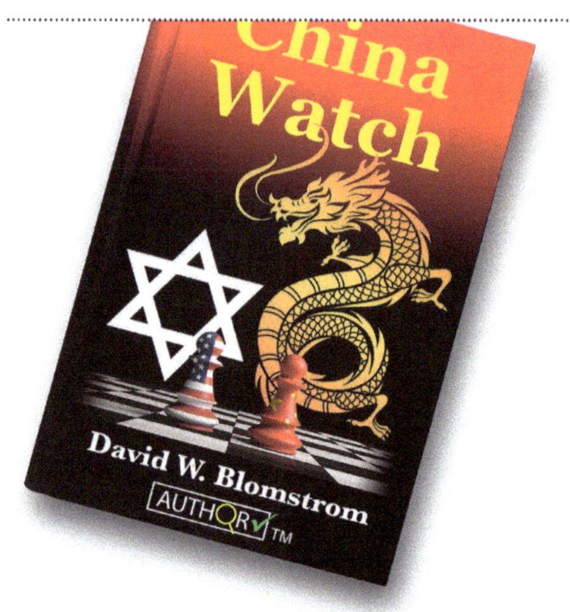

To learn more about my China Watch and Conspiracy Science series, vist ChinaWatch.Pro and Conspiracy1.com. There you can learn about other books that make up the most amazing underground library you will ever discover.

If, by chance, you have an interest in state symbols (e.g. state flags, flowers, birds, etc.), then check out Geobop's Symbols (symbols.geobop.com). I'm working on a series of books focusing on state symbols, including by far the biggest, most complete reference ever published. The series is surprisingly political (or not).